Aspects of Ageing

edited by

Peter Kaim-Caudle, Jane Keithley and Audrey Mullender

Whiting & Birch Ltd
MCMXCIII

Published by Whiting & Birch Ltd,
PO Box 872, Forest Hill, London SE23 3HL, England.
USA: Paul & Co, Publishers' Consortium Inc,
PO Box 442, Concord, MA 017422.

British Library Cataloguing in Publication Data.
A CIP catalogue record is available from the British Library

ISBN 1 871177 57 X (cased)
ISBN 1 871177 58 8 (limp)

Printed in England by Bourne Press, Bournemouth

Aspects of Ageing

Contents

Acknowledgements

This book is the product of the initiative taken by the University of Durham's Centre for Applied Social Studies and Institute of Health Studies in asking Peter Kaim-Caudle to organise a series of seminars and public lectures in support of the 1993 European Year of Older People and Solidarity Between Generations (EYOP).

We are grateful to the contributors and to David Boyes, the designer of the front cover of the book, all of whom donated their services in support of the Year. We also acknowledge with thanks the financial support we have received from the University's Public Lectures Committee and from EYOP-Durham.

The project was much assisted by the cooperation of the Durham County Council's Department of Social Services (Director, Peter Kemp) and the Department of Arts, Libraries and Museums (Director, Patrick Conway).

Lastly, we thank John Thornberry, the chairman of EYOP-Durham and the Durham County Coordinator of Community Care, and Nigel Canaway, the treasurer of EYOP-Durham and Special Services Manager of the Department of Arts, Libraries and Museums, who served on our editorial committee. They have greatly contributed to bringing the University's support of EYOP to the attention of many citizens of County Durham as part of their outstanding commitment to the objectives of this celebratory year.

Introduction

AUDREY MULLENDER AND JANE KEITHLEY

This publication arises from two series of events held in Durham to mark the European Year of Older People and Solidarity Between Generations (EYOP). Jointly organised by EYOP-Durham and the University of Durham, these were a programme of ten seminars on the theme of 'ageing and society' presented by locally based scholars and a series of four public lectures by speakers of international prominence. All took the European Year as their topic.

Of the fifteen contributors to the book, including the editors, eleven have a past or present connection with the University of Durham, including Chris Phillipson who gained his doctorate there. The quality and substance of the papers given at both the lectures and the seminars were of such a high standard that it was decided to offer them as a tribute to the European Year, in the form of the present publication.

The collection was not planned as a comprehensive coverage of the topic of ageing - which, since it embraces elements of the whole of human life, would be hard to encompass - but provides a great many intriguing insights. A number of the contributors are themselves advanced in years and bring a life-time's reflection and learning to their specialist areas of interest, as well as a personal perspective on ageing. The title of this collection, *Aspects of Ageing* , is intended to reflect, on the one hand, its variety and, on the other, our recognition that these were but a selection of personal and professional viewpoints; this is not a commissioned set of interlocking studies. Indeed, none of the authors was given a title or a topic to address. Each made her or his own choice of focus and approach.

This strength, in drawing on the interest and specialist expertise of individuals, is also a limitation. For example, we are aware that ethnic issues are not given the prominence they deserve in the collection as a whole. For someone who experiences old age as a Moslem in Bosnia or as a Turk in Germany - or as an African Caribbean or South Asian person in Britain, come to that - the issues raised in growing older and in daily living are often very different. We welcome the discussion of some of these issues at other events mounted during the European year (see, for example, *Race, Migration and Older People in Europe: Conference Report*, forthcoming from Lanpol at the University of Central Lancashire).

Although this book is a collection of individually chosen topics, a number of identifiable themes run through the chapters: in particular, those of the Year itself in celebrating the lives of older people, the solidarity which can be found between the generations, and the experience of growing older in a specifically European context. It also achieves a certain 'wholeness' - like the fulfilment of a long life - through the physical, social, cultural, intellectual and spiritual elements of its multi-disciplinary content.

European Focus

The chapters with the most specifically European focus are those by Alan Walker and Ilona Ostner. Alan Walker is one of a small group of European Community experts on ageing drawn together for the Year. He engagingly summarises some of the findings of the 1993 report from the European Observatory, on social and economic policies for older people in Europe, together with the Eurobarometer's survey of attitudes towards ageing held by older and younger age-groups. As one would expect, these studies investigated issues of financial well-being, the impact of pensions systems, and the provision of social care services. However, they also touched on questions revealing deep-seated cultural and social attitudes, such as what generic term older people in each of the member states would choose for themselves (the British prefer 'senior citizens'), whether there are hostile feelings between the generations (in the main there are not), whether older people feel lonely (surprisingly, this is more common in the southern states of Europe), the rise of pensioners' movements, and the potential for combating age discrimination at national and international level.

No collection on an ageing population could afford to ignore women, given their greater average longevity compared to men. Ilona Ostner is an eminent commentator upon the social policy of Europe. Throughout her career, she has made a special study of gender issues and in her chapter she challenges the European Community to extend its consideration of equity and justice towards older women and informal carers. She sees both paid work and unpaid caring, increasingly combined in women's lives, as embedded within 'a complex system of subordination and precedence'. Drawing comparisons and contrasts from every part of Europe, she demonstrates that a range of welfare traditions all tend to disadvantage women, though to a varying degree and in a variety of ways.

The Themes of Old Age and Generational Solidarity

Many of the authors represented in this book have written from the perspective of their discipline, rather than as specialists in gerontology. Chris Phillipson is the most notable exception. He has devoted his career to the study of this complex, rapidly expanding, and in many ways most neglected of all the ages. His chapter clearly demonstrates that older people no longer, in any sense, constitute one 'age'. All European and many other countries now contain large numbers of people right through the span from 55, 60 or 65 (whichever threshold is chosen) to the growing number of centenarians. The wide age range means that even the concepts of a 'third' and 'fourth' age are now inadequate.

Many people, especially women, can now expect one quarter to one third of their life-span to extend beyond the official retirement age and the end of child-rearing. They do not form a homogeneous group but a many faceted and large segment of the population with a multiplicity of interests, needs and strengths, cultural and social backgrounds, abilities and disabilities. Chris Phillipson demonstrates the tension between traditional capitalist views of retired people as a burden, and the enormously increased opportunities which ought now to be available to enable people to experience a rich and long life well after paid work ends. His chapter also reverses the field-glass to look at society from an older person's perspective, and poses important questions as yet untouched by detailed research, such as the nature of intimacy and sexuality in old age, of choice in relationships between the generations, and of daily life in late old age.

Reminding us that the European Year concentrated not only on older people but on 'solidarity between generations', Bill Williamson takes as his theme the changing patterns of relationships between the generations in contemporary European societies. He argues that there is a subtle bond between the oldest and the youngest age-groups, that their fates are linked, and that they have mutual concerns: for example, in bearing disproportionately the costs of social and economic restructuring. However, this bond is being eroded by growing inequalities and ageist thinking; processes which it needs a conscious decision to reverse.

An Ageing Population

The economists and demographers in the collection, all from Durham, are concerned with age relationships in a different sense as they draw in the social backcloth of Britain's ageing population. The demographic picture is painted with precision and clarity by John Clarke. His chapter, 'European population structures', brings together examples from all parts of Europe and includes occasional illustrations from County Durham. In 'Why so many old?', Peter Kaim-Caudle expands on this theme and looks for answers. Between 1901 and 1991, the total population of England and Wales increased by half, while the number of elderly people increased five fold. Unpicking the demographic figures to tease out precisely why there are now more 'very elderly' and more female elderly in the UK population, he concludes that future changes in fertility will be a more important determinant of the size and age composition of the population than changes in mortality. In 'Economic implications of ageing', Barry Thomas looks at the changing age composition from an economist's point of view. His chapter includes consideration of the increased burden on the working population of sustaining the generations beyond retirement age. He discusses, too, the impact of an ageing population on savings and the shift in expenditure to goods and services bought by older people. Finally, a comparison is made between public expenditure which benefits old people with that which benefits children.

Community Care

In 1993, one might have been forgiven for equating old age solely with the topic of community care, since this year is also notable for the implementation of a major shake-up in health and social services. Chapters reflecting the response of these sectors to older people are those by Margot Jefferys, Yvette Marin and Lorna Warren. Margot Jefferys is a distinguished medical sociologist. In 'Is there a need for geriatric medicine?', she contrasts, on the one hand, the advances in specialist care, teamwork and community focus achieved by having separated off the health care of elderly people in the UK with, on the other, the low status of the specialism and its rigid demarcation by age rather than degree or nature of illness. In her verbal presentation, she came down on the side of retaining the targeted resources represented by geriatric medicine and commented on the envy of those concerned with health care in other European nations which did not elect to divide services in this way.

The chapter by Yvette Marin is the only one in the book that has yet to be delivered as a paper in Durham. Conscious that the collection tends otherwise towards the anglocentric, we welcomed the opportunity to be transported into the dining-room of a sheltered housing complex, the dormitory of a large institution, and the living-room of a private apartment in France. This crucial detail of the quality of daily life is set within the context of a major debate about the future of health and social care provision for older people in that country. This echoes many of the concerns being faced all over Europe as it contrasts community integration with professional care, public policies with private preferences, and co-ordinated planning with local traditions and a diversifying economy of welfare.

Also in this area of debate, is a contribution on 'Implementing community care' by Lorna Warren. Taking involvement and participation as her themes, she tackles ageism head on. Using the example of domiciliary services for older people with high care needs, she argues that services still fall far short of ensuring that the views and preferences of service users are respected and taken into account in assessment of need, choice of services or service review. She concludes by suggesting how the participation of older people in services might be improved.

The Wider Perspective

Attitudes towards older people through the centuries can be traced most effectively, perhaps, in literature. In 'Ageing in literature', Roger Till moves us from the social sciences to the humanities to take a broader perspective. He uses a wide-ranging selection of quotations from our English heritage to illustrate different images of, and perspectives on, ageing and older people.

There are vivid images, too, in 'Social participation in old age'. Here, Robin Humphrey reminds us that Durham is not only a cathedral and a university; another great tradition of the county is coal-mining. He describes the findings of an oral history project which sought to capture and preserve for posterity older women's memories of their lives in a former mining village in County Durham. These were miners' wives of a different generation: not standing on the picket line but dedicating themselves to the home - their own and, in their youth, their employers'. Here, they are portrayed in their later years, enjoying a well earned social life and looking back on years of love, hardship and neighbourliness. Though 1993 will also be remembered as the year the last pit closed in County Durham, the special spirit of the Miners' Gala reminded us that the village, the people, and the pride are still there.

Wherever one turns in Durham, one is watched over by that great cathedral. It is perhaps not surprising, then, that our thoughts in assembling this collection turned also to matters spiritual, though from a quite different tradition. In 'Dying: an eastern perspective', Brian Holton explores the process of dying from the perspective of Tibetan Buddhist practices with specific reference to the *Book of the Dead*. The attempt is made to set these ideas within the broader context of Buddhist psychology and philosophy - and to suggest that engaging with them might help us redefine our own concepts of death and dying. Finally, we look outwards in another way, to end with 'Speculating about the future' by Peter Kaim-Caudle. In addition to pensions and health care, trends towards fragmenting community services, costs borne by service users, and official opposition to legislative action on age discrimination are examined. The conclusion is reached that the well-being of older people in the UK over the next thirty years will be more determined by political decisions, at national and European level, than by the imperatives of demography.

A Wide Audience

The presentations gathered together here reached a mixed audience of professionals, academics and the general public - both young and old. Older people themselves represent a more diverse group than ever before in history. We look forward to this book reaching a similarly broad readership.

Older people in Europe: perceptions and realities

ALAN WALKER

This paper reports the findings of two major pieces of work mounted by the European Community for 1993, the European Year of Older People and Solidarity Between the Generations. First, a Eurobarometer survey of public attitudes to ageing and older people.[1] There were in fact two surveys: one of the general public aged 15 and over and the other of older people. The findings from these unique surveys provide us with the first comprehensive picture both of how older people in Europe are perceived and, in turn, how they themselves perceive the ageing process. Of course we must be cautious about what is essentially public opinion poll data, but this is the only information of its kind that we have.

Secondly, the EC's Observatory on Ageing and Older People has produced the most definitive report yet written on social and economic policy issues affecting older people in the member states. The report, based on the research of the twelve national experts in the Observatory, provides objective data on the social and economic status of older people as well as detailed policy analysis with which we can compare the opinions and perceptions collected by the Eurobarometer surveys.[2]

This short paper concentrates on five key policy issues by way of illustrating the main findings from this recent work: relations between the generations, living standards, employment, intra-family relationships and social care, and the 'politics' of ageing.

Inter-Generational Relations

First there is the issue that lies at the heart of this European Year and, arguably, is fundamental to all human societies: relations between the generations. Literature is scattered with references to this issue - Job and his sons, Oedipus, King Lear and his untrustworthy daughters - so this is an age old question. In the Eurobarometer survey, we sought to establish the current state of relations between the generations in EC countries.

We found that older people are favourably inclined towards the young - regarding young people on the whole as being helpful towards older people. There are national variations: in Denmark and Ireland older people are most positive about youth and in Belgium and Italy they are least positive. But in no EC country is there any indication of strong antagonism of older people towards younger ones.

Also, we found some striking similarities in opinions between younger and older people and in the major political issues they espouse - which contradicts the popular perception of a generation gap.

There is quite a high level of interaction between younger and older people, with over one-third of senior citizens in the EC as a whole reporting a lot of contact with those under 25. When asked if they want more contact with younger people there was a clear division between the North and South of the Community: older people in the South - Greece, Italy and Portugal - said they wanted more contact; while those in the North - Denmark, the Netherlands and the UK - said they did not.

There were warning signals, however. For example in the survey of general public opinion there was a majority who thought that older people are not admired and respected by younger people; there was also a majority who felt that older people are too set in their ways and ideas, too conservative or inflexible. But the overall impression is one of healthy intergenerational relations. This was confirmed when we asked whether older and younger people should mix together more often socially - the response was almost unanimous, with nine out of ten respondents saying yes, they should.

So far I have focused on micro-sociological interpersonal relationships, but what about the big macro-policy issue concerning intergenerational relations: the funding of pensions? There has been a great deal of debate in all member states about the implications of population ageing for pension systems, including much political rhetoric about dependency ratios and the burden of pensions. Some countries have taken steps to curtail the growth of pension spending - the UK, Germany and Italy - while others are contemplating such changes.

Underlying all pension systems is a contract between the generations: the working population contributes towards the pensions of those in retirement. Therefore it is vital to know whether or not the general public is willing to go on paying for pensions. To test this we asked whether or not those in employment have a duty to ensure, through the taxes or contributions they pay, that older people have a decent standard of living. The results show a remarkably high level of positive consensus, right across the EC, with some four out of five people on average and never less than seven out of ten agreeing with the proposition. This indicates that the social contract - the most critical test of intergenerational relations - is not just alive and well, but apparently in a very healthy state.

Thus the common perception of both a growing generational gap in outlook and, perhaps more importantly, of increasing tensions and possibly open conflict between workers and pensioners is simply not borne out by the facts and the opinions of those involved. There are two clear messages for policy-makers: firstly, beware of rhetoric emphasising generational conflict, as this may help to create a problem that does not exist at present; and secondly, it is important to examine the impact of policies on generational relations - they are precious and we must take care not to damage them.

Living Standards

I turn secondly to the issue that is of most immediate concern to older people themselves: their standard of living. Financial security is the cornerstone of social integration in EC countries, therefore this policy issue features centrally in both the Eurobarometer and Observatory reports.

Incomes and living standards raise some of the most difficult and controversial questions concerning the impact of social and economic policies on older people. It is not possible in this brief paper to go into much detail (there are extensive analyses of the key issues in Chapter 2 of the Observatory's report). Instead I will concentrate on a simple triad: the subjective perceptions of first the general public and secondly, older people themselves, and then contrast these thirdly, with the objective analyses contained in the Observatory's research.

Let us consider the perceptions of the general public first. When EC citizens were asked about the main problems facing older people in their country, two issues were mentioned more than any others: financial difficulties and loneliness. Of the two, financial problems were the most frequently mentioned - with an EC average of just under one in two people saying they regarded this as the main problem facing older people in their country. There were wide variations between countries from a low of 23 per cent in Luxembourg, followed closely by 26 per cent in Denmark to a high of 72 per cent in Portugal - the next highest was the UK with 66 per cent.

Turning, secondly, to older people themselves, we asked them to describe their current financial situation. The majority feel that they are getting by, with care. Very few described themselves as very comfortable financially. In fact in most countries only a minority of senior citizens regard themselves as either comfortable financially or very comfortable. The three main exceptions are Denmark, Luxembourg and the Netherlands, where something like a 'culture of financial contentment' may be witnessed.

Social gerontologists have long been aware of an apparent paradox whereby older people who, by objective criteria, are suffering poverty and deprivation may nonetheless express, subjectively, satisfaction with their living standards. Further analysis of the survey results will allow us to test this paradox on a European scale. For the moment it is important to establish that, by a large majority, older people regard themselves as financially secure. Of course there were variations between member states - a high of 89 per cent in Denmark and a low of 40 per cent in Greece - and within one of them - 78 per cent in the former FDR compared with 57 per cent in the former GDR - but overall more than seven out of ten older Europeans said they were financially secure. So, regardless of the objective situation, there is no sign of widespread feelings of financial insecurity on the part of older people.

Those in the general population survey that had retired were asked whether the pensions (public and private) they receive are adequate. The responses divide the Community into three groups: those countries where a large majority of older people regard their pensions as adequate (Denmark, Germany, Luxembourg and the Netherlands); those where opinion is split on adequacy versus inadequacy (Belgium, France, Ireland, Italy, Spain and the UK); and those where large majorities say pensions are inadequate (Greece and Portugal). This evidence is not concerned with objective measures, but viewed from the perspective of those on the receiving end, the EC's pension systems are not entirely successful. It is only in four member states that most older people seem to be satisfied with their pensions.

The results of a second question to pensioners in the main Eurobarometer survey seem to indicate a relatively high level of frustrated aspirations and perhaps even latent resentment over the level of pensions people had accrued when in employment. We asked them to take into account the contributions they had made during their working lives and then to say whether the pension they now receive allows them to lead the life they would like to lead.

Only just over one in eight were definitely positive in their response to this question and the most certain were in Denmark (34 per cent) and Luxembourg (39 per cent). Adding together those who said yes definitely and those who said probably, there were what we might call satisfied majorities in Belgium, Denmark, Luxembourg and the Netherlands. Thus in Denmark, Luxembourg and the Netherlands there appears to be a high level of contentment, on the part of pensioners, with the level of the pensions they receive, as both a source of income and a well-earned reward for a working life. The countries in which older people were most definite that their pensions do not produce the living standards they would like after a life-time's contributions are in, descending order: Greece (66 per cent), Portugal (56 per cent), Italy and Spain (42 per cent) and the UK (41 per cent).

Turning, thirdly, to the objective evidence (drawing on the Observatory's work) there are obvious contradictions between this expert analysis and the perceptions of both the general public and older people. Before looking at the evidence it is important to note the point made by virtually every national expert: there is a distinct lack of detailed information on the living standards of older people. This applies to both northern and southern states. For example the author of the German report comments that 'figures on the actual income situation of older people are unfortunately in scarce supply. The official statistics do not provide the relevant information on a regular basis'. This widespread deficiency in statistics about the living standards of older people is of the utmost importance in policy terms, because it suggests that policy makers do not have access to the information necessary to make informed judgements about priorities. It is hoped that one result of the European Year will be better information about the social conditions of this large and growing segment of EC citizens. If older people are to be full citizens of the Community policy makers must be better informed about their living conditions.

The information that is available indicates that there are four key features of recent developments in the objective living standards of senior citizens.

First, in a majority of EC countries, the average incomes of older people have risen in recent years along with those of the population as a whole. However it is only in a minority of member states that this is the result of positive action by governments to improve the position of older people. Examples of such positive action include the French government's extension of the coverage of social assistance and indexation of pensions; the Grand Duchy of Luxembourg's recently introduced National Programme for Older People; and the Spanish government's policy of raising minimum pension levels. In the majority of countries, however, rising average living standards are the result of increases in the scope and coverage of occupational pensions or pension scheme maturation. This means that the impact is uneven on senior citizens - those with access to occupational pensions have prospered while those reliant on minimal state pensions have fallen behind. It is often the case that the younger pensioners have benefited from developments in occupational pensions while the older ones have not.

Secondly, there are wide variations in the levels of pensions in different member states. The most commonly used measure of pension levels is the replacement ratio - the amount of the pensions an individual receives compared with their last earned income. This is the comparison alluded to in Paragraph 24 of the Charter of the Fundamental Social Rights of Workers. However, recently released Eurostat data show that the goal of full replacement is far from being achieved in several member states and, for a married pensioner whose salary when in employment was equal to average earnings and who had contributed to pension schemes for a full term (35-45 years), his pensions as a percentage of his previous earnings range from just over 60 per cent in two countries to over 90 per cent in four member states.

Thirdly, despite rising living standards, the national reports of Observatory members reveal a continuing problem of poverty among a minority of older people. Research by the Observatory reveals a wide range of experience among the member states in the extent of their success in protecting senior citizens from poverty. The poverty rates among older people in some countries are between five and seven times greater than those in others. At one end of the spectrum the author of the Germany report, Jens Alber, states that 'German pensioners are better described as living in relative affluence than as living in relative poverty'; while at the other, Heloisa Perista, our Portuguese expert, comments that 'A great majority of old age pensioners are particularly vulnerable to the incidence of poverty'. These differences in experience between senior citizens in two different parts of the EC stretch the notion of Community to its very limit and, in doing so, pose a challenge to policy makers to ensure the realisation of the EC's goal of economic security in old age in all member states.

Fourthly, regardless of a nation's success in reducing poverty in old age there are continuing differences in living standards among pensioners and in some cases these are widening. The primary inequalities are based on age and gender and, of course, the interaction between the two. On the one hand there are inequalities in income between the recently retired and older age groups, the third and fourth ages. On the other hand women are more likely to live longer and are less likely to have full pension contribution records in employment and, therefore, they are more likely than men to be poor in old age. These generational and gender inequalities represent serious fault lines in the pensions and social protection systems of the majority of member states. They seem to be indicative, not simply of the lack of adequate protection given to certain groups of older people from bearing a disproportionate share of deprivation and the need for additional policy measures, but, more fundamentally, they suggest that some of the policies themselves may have contributed to the problem.

Generational inequalities

In all EC countries except Denmark, inequalities may be observed between younger and older age groups of pensioners (even in Denmark there is a tendency for very elderly women to be poorer than other groups). There are some signs of a separation between younger and older pensioners - 'two nations' in old age - in some EC countries, though the general picture is not one of sharp polarisation between them. However, what can be said with certainty is that there are generational inequalities in income in eleven out of twelve member states, but also that there are substantial differences in the degree of these income inequalities between countries. The one member state to escape this trend so far, Denmark, is likely to emulate it in future.

On the basis of incomplete data it is not possible to categorise all countries, even crudely. However it is possible to distinguish between countries, such as France and Ireland, where generational inequalities appear to be relatively narrow and are not increasing and those, like Belgium, Greece, the Netherlands, Portugal, Spain and the UK, where they are relatively wide. (No age-related data are available for Germany but, taking the older population as a whole the German report notes a 'fairly high degree of inequality' around a large middle income group.) It is also possible to observe trends in two of these contrasting member states.

In France, for example, the picture is one of relatively narrow and narrowing generational inequalities. However, despite the relatively narrow generational inequalities in France, the older age groups are still more likely to rely predominantly on pension income and, therefore, have to have recourse to social assistance. Thus 55 per cent of those in their 80s receive a pension worth less than the old age minimum benefit from the FNS compared with 21 per cent of those in their sixties.

In contrast, in neighbouring Belgium, the risk of poverty (in 1985) was more than three times higher in the 75 and over age group than in the 50-64 group and the probability of experiencing long term poverty three times higher. In Spain those aged 80 and over are more than twice as likely as 60-64 year olds and twice as likely as 65-79 year olds to have very low incomes (less than 20,000 pesetas - 144 ECUs - a month).

Turning now to trends in generational income differences in old age, the position of France is one of narrowing inequalities between age groups with pension system maturation. In contrast, in Belgium, new dynamic data for the period 1985-88 shows that income inequalities in old age are widening. In fact, remarkably, inequalities in income among the economically active and between the active and retired have remained constant and, therefore, the growth in income differences between the third (50-74) and fourth (75 and over) ages has produced an overall increase in inequality for the population as a whole. In the UK the arrival of a significant group of relatively affluent older people, quite distinct from the middle income and poor groups, has created the acronym WOOPIE to denote better-off, largely younger, elderly people or third agers. The term 'WOOPIE' has also been used in Belgium. Looking at the EC as a whole it appears that the cases of narrowing generational inequalities (France, Germany and Ireland) are the exceptions rather than the rule.

Gender inequalities

Linked partly to generational or age-cohort divisions there are differences between male and female pensioners in income and living standards. This issue emerges from virtually every national report as being one of the most pressing ones facing policy makers. The main exception, yet again, is Denmark, though even in that country there is a tendency among single people over 80 for men to have higher incomes than women.

Even in the French case where generational differences are narrowing among both men and women, the division in pension levels between men and women has actually increased. Recipients of the means-tested minimum FNS are more likely to be women than men. Likewise, in Italy, the median sum of old age pensions of women is 67 per cent of the male median. In Germany the average pension paid to women in 1990 was just 42 per cent of the male average. In 1989 women formed 76 per cent of social assistance recipients aged 60 and over and 83 per cent of those aged 75 and over.

Similar data could be adduced for Luxembourg, the

Netherlands, Portugal, Spain and the UK showing that the average incomes of older women are low relative to other younger groups and to older men. The consistency of this finding across virtually the whole of the EC is remarkable: older women, particularly widows, comprise some of the poorest and most socially excluded groups in the Community both north and south - a phenomenon sometimes referred to as the feminisation of poverty in old age.

In Ireland, however, households headed by older women are at a low risk of poverty relative to other age categories, particularly older men (for instance 13 per cent of men aged 65 years or over are below the 50 per cent of average disposable income poverty line compared to 5 per cent of women). One possible explanation for this may be the relatively high proportion of elderly men engaged in farming, an activity that has been identified as carrying a higher risk of poverty compared to other labour force categories.

Policy implications

To some extent these observed differences in income between pensioners, based on both age and gender, are a product of social and economic policies. This is not surprising, given the reliance of older people on pension systems, but nonetheless it requires some explanation. It is not simply the case that policies have not been applied fully to the problems of socio-economic and gender inequalities in the labour market, though that is a major factor explaining continuing economic insecurity among older women in most countries, but in some cases the policies themselves have helped to create or more usually to have perpetuated such differences.

Widening inequalities in income between pensioners are of vital importance, in policy terms, for two reasons. First, they may be a wholly unintended by-product of improvements in pension systems. Paradoxically, by concentrating on the newly retired or the future pensions of those currently in the labour market, the needs of those who have already retired may be neglected to some extent. Secondly, in some countries it is clear that deprivation is heavily concentrated, by the coincidence of generational and gender inequalities, on very elderly women.

Dealing first with age-cohort or generational differences, policy makers in some countries have relied on pension scheme maturation and the growth of occupational and private pensions to improve the living standards of pensioners. But these policies inevitably disadvantage older cohorts of pensioners. The problem was succinctly summarised by the authors of the French report (in translation):

Each generation leaving working life has found better conditions than the generations preceding it; that is why the younger the pensioners are today, the higher are their pensions.

Turning, secondly, to the related gender inequalities in income, these in some cases appear to be even more intractable. However, since an important source of such differences in the living standards of men and women is the pension systems themselves and, specifically, the way they interact with the labour market, they must be amenable to policy reform. The main causal factors are that women's employment patterns differ from men's and, crucially, that the majority of the pension systems in the EC are founded on an employment-testing and/or earnings equivalence requirement. Thus, under both flat-rate and earnings-related basic pension schemes, a contribution record must be built-up in employment. Similarly with supplementary occupational pensions a contribution record must be established to be entitled to one, and part-time workers (predominantly female) are usually not allowed to participate in such pensions or to do so on the same basis as full-time employees. Such 'male-orientated' requirements inevitably disadvantage women.

Having looked at the three elements of the living standards triad - public perceptions, the opinions of older people and objective statistical data and expert analysis - we may bring them all together by referring back to the Eurobarometer study. Not surprisingly those EC countries with the lowest poverty rates also tend to have the most contented pensioners and vice versa.

We also asked about the level of income that should be provided by the state to older people. The results reveal strong support in the member states for the public provision of a decent standard of living for older people. The majority of EC citizens believe that older people should have incomes close to average wages rather than at subsistence level.

What about the vexed question of paying for pensions? We tackled this question head-on in the Eurobarometer surveys.

The results reveal a clear distinction between the general public's opinion on the pensions/taxation equation in those countries with pension levels in the top half of the EC league as compared to those in the bottom half. The former (e.g. Denmark, Germany, France, Belgium) are more likely to have said that pension levels are about right or that they are too low but will have to stay at that level, while the latter (e.g. Greece, Spain, Portugal, UK) are more likely to have said that they are too low and should be raised even if this means increasing contributions or taxes. The former FDR and GDR were found to be on opposite sides of the divide. The minuscule proportions in every member state of people saying that pensions are too high are striking - there is widespread agreement that pensions are not too high.

So, the results of the two reports show that perceptions and reality are synchronised to some extent. The main exception is the relatively high proportion of older people who regard their pension as adequate despite objective evidence to the contrary. This seems to pose a huge political challenge to those organisations in Europe that are trying to mobilise senior citizens. The Eurobarometer survey also revealed quite a high level of pessimism among the general public about how far the pensions contract will be honoured in the future - over half believing that they will get less pensions for their contributions in the future.

Employment

The main point to make with respect to employment is that the Eurobarometer study reveals a considerable difference in perceptions between the general public and policy makers.

Early labour force exit has been the dominant characteristic of the labour market experience of older workers over the last 20 years. In some countries, including the UK, policies have openly encouraged older workers to leave the labour market, particularly at times of high youth unemployment. Indeed there has been a tendency for policy makers to regard early retirement as a cure for unemployment.

So we asked the general public whether people in their 50s should give up work to make way for young people? The response was remarkable - on average two-thirds said that they should not. Moreover there was hardly any difference between younger people and older ones in the answers they gave.

Policy makers in most EC countries have been reluctant to recognise - in law or policy - the existence of age discrimination. But an extraordinarily high proportion of citizens in all EC countries believe that older workers are discriminated against with regard to job recruitment (79 per cent), promotion (62 per cent) and training (67 per cent). Again there were hardly any differences between age-groups: both young and old believe that discrimination against older workers is commonplace. Hard evidence is difficult to come by, but the Observatory experts have looked at the issue of age discrimination and there is no doubt that it exists. Thus popular perceptions and expert analysis coincide.

Finally the public were asked if the government of their country should or should not introduce laws to combat age discrimination. By a large majority of two to one EC citizens favour such government action. There were clear majorities in every country apart from Denmark.

Social Care

Increased longevity is a sign of social and economic progress, including the successful intervention in death and disease by public health measures. However this means that there are more and more people who are likely to need some level of personal care or support. This realisation sometimes leads to the conclusion that all older people require care. Nothing could be further from the truth. The reality is that most older people are relatively fit, healthy and able to look after themselves or to do so with only minimal assistance. Moreover if help is required it usually comes first from the family (female kin in particular) - in the majority of EC countries the state plays a minor role in the care of older people, either as a direct provider or funder of care. However, the need for care is rising and various changes in family composition and behaviour are restricting the supply of informal carers. This raises a number of crucial policy issues.

Chief among them is the extent to which the family will remain the primary source of care for older people. As noted above all of the evidence - including the Observatory and Eurobarometer - shows the crucial role of the family in the care of older people but, nonetheless a perception has arisen that the family is less willing to care for its relatives than it used to be. The Eurobarometer survey found that this view is prevalent among older people themselves: one third agreed strongly and one third slightly that families are less willing to care for older relatives than they used to be. This finding is of the utmost importance because it points to a worrying perception among senior citizens, even if there is no objective evidence to support it. Or, at least, there is no evidence of a reduction in willingness but, as a result of the changes taking place in family structure it is less able to care in some circumstances.

The objective evidence about social contacts between older people and their families shows that there are frequent face-to-face interactions. On average nearly four out of five older people see a member of their family at least once a week. Nearly three out of four see a friend at least once a week. So the idea that older people have been abandoned by their families is a myth. However there is a significant minority who suffer from loneliness and wide variations in this experience between member states, particularly on the North/South axis: less than 5 per cent of older people in Denmark report feeling lonely often, compared with over 20 per cent in Portugal and Greece.

There is also the claim sometimes made that the state is taking over caring responsibilities from the family. In reality there is a completely different relationship between the state and the family: as people become very elderly and begin to lose close relatives, the role of the public social services increases - in other words, they are complementary. Though this statement must be qualified by the observation that, in reality, it is only a minority of EC countries that have an extensive range of social services in which they can play a fully complementary role. For example in Denmark more than two-thirds of those in the Eurobarometer survey who were receiving care were being assisted by the social services. Next came the Netherlands and the UK with just over one-quarter receiving such help; followed by Belgium and France with just under one-fifth. After that all of the percentages were in single figures.

The final issue concerning care is that of residential versus community care. When the general public in each member state was asked about the most appropriate place for care to be provided to older people, the vast majority (four out of five) thought that older people should be helped to remain in their own homes. This indicates that there is very strong support for community care among EC citizens. Older people too favour this option. Not surprisingly, as the costs of residential care have risen, more and more policy makers have become interested in community care. So there is a common perception that this is the right policy.

The problem is that when we examine the objective reality, as the Observatory has done, we find first of all that recent reductions in long-stay facilities have not been matched by an expansion in home care, and secondly that social services are failing to keep pace with the needs created by ageing populations. As it happens the two countries with the most extensive home care services - Denmark and the Netherlands - are also those with the largest residential care sectors. The provision of community care facilities in other countries is less extensive and experts point to frequent care gaps - where the supply of care is not keeping pace with the demand for it. More worrying still is the fact that recent reductions in home care services are reported in several countries.

So, there is a large gap in some countries between political rhetoric about the importance of community care and the actual supply of services, even though there is common ground between the public, older people and policy makers about the importance of this policy.

The Politics of Ageing

Lastly I turn to some general issues concerning the politics of old age - what roles should older people occupy in modern European society? The answers to this question are of great importance, not least to those representing older people on the European stage.

I will start on what seems to be a lighter note but actually goes to the very heart of how older people are treated in society and what role they want to occupy: what this group of people is called by the rest of us. This is important because names carry symbolic meanings, they tell us a great deal about the social status of the labelled. The most commonly used label for older people is 'elderly' and this suggests a passive, retiring perception of the group and also that they are a separate group from the rest of society.

We asked older people in the Eurobarometer survey the direct question: what do you prefer to be called? The answers were revealing: they show that older people, on the whole, reject the passive perception of themselves as 'elderly'. They prefer labels such as 'older people' which implies that they are like the rest of us, only older, or 'senior citizens' which carries connotations of individuals as civic actors, with rights and duties and, therefore, stresses the integration of older people rather than their separation.

It is worth noting that older people rejected the media image of a 'golden age' with its suggestion of comfortable affluence. This surely is a sign of the clash of such romantic perceptions with the, often harsh, reality of the lives of older people. However, above all, older Europeans seem to be telling us that they want to be regarded as citizens like the rest of the community.

Pursuing this theme, it is the case that both popular media images and literary portrayals of older people are often passive ones (e.g. Shakespeare's seven ages of man or W.B. Yeat's poem on old age). But the evidence from the Eurobarometer survey shows that the reality is quite different. The real picture is that older people in many EC countries are active citizens: on average two out of three are either very busy or leading full lives.

This positive image must be qualified in two respects. First there are significant differences between two southern states - Greece and Portugal - and the rest of the Community. It is a sad fact that one in five in Greece and one in seven in Portugal said that they either have too much time on their hands or have nothing to do. Research by the Observatory shows that policy makers are aware of this problem but there is clearly a need for more action.

Secondly, when it comes to political activity, the popular perception is correct: older people do appear to be passive. Only just over one in a hundred had taken part in political or pressure group activities in the previous seven days. This does not mean that older Europeans are not interested in politics but they are not often active participants.

As far as the general public is concerned this state of affairs is undesirable - they want the reality to change. For example a large majority of the public in the member states say that older people are not represented fully enough on radio and television. The public is also unanimous that older people should stand up more actively for their rights.

It is worth noting, finally, that national governments and the EC itself are out of step with public opinion. More than three out of four of all EC citizens sampled think that their government does not do enough for older people and just under three out of five say that the EC should do more for this group.

Conclusion

This summary of some information in the Eurobarometer and Observatory reports shows that there are some key variations between EC states in the social conditions experienced by older people - variations that undermine the notion of Community and therefore act as a policy challenge to the EC, particularly in this European Year.

But perhaps the two main messages to emerge from the two reports I have been reviewing are, first, that most EC countries have not fully adjusted to the fact that they are ageing societies. Policies and perceptions have not caught up with the reality of rising numbers of older people, which means profound changes in our societies: more resources for pensions and health and social care, new attitudes in the labour market, in families and elsewhere, including a new politics of old age. Secondly, the two reports demonstrate the immense value of sharing experiences between the member states, so that they can learn from each other. This is a powerful demonstration of the positive benefits of the European Community. But this European Year marks the end of the current programme and we have only just started the task of sharing knowledge and experience in this field.

This paper was delivered at Durham University, 12 May 1993

References

1. Walker, A. *Age and Attitudes*. Brussels: EC Commission.
2. Walker, A., Guillemard, A-M. and Alber, J. *Older People in Europe - Social and Economic Policies*. Brussels: EC Commission.

Whose solidarity with whom?
The case of women in
old age in the European Community

ILONA OSTNER

Introduction

European integration and its impact on a country's wealth, well-being and welfare culture have been much talked about. Issues, however, which do not link easily with the functioning of a common market - like age and caring for frail elderly people - have remained at the margin. How does the Community take into account that all her citizens are gendered and embedded in generation? What can elderly women hope to gain from the European Community (EC)?

The EC has been primarily concerned with creating a common market. Policies have been aimed at removing obstacles to free trade and mobility of labour within the market. Women's concerns, therefore, are considered only from a strict market angle (Raasch, 1990, p.64). They have to be translated into specific employment issues if women want to profit from EC policy. During their lives, however, women move constantly between employment and unpaid domestic work. Unlike men, many women work part-time and intermittently. As a result, their concerns cross-cut the boundaries between the private domestic sphere and the public one of state and market.

Whether women profit from an emerging Social Europe will depend on the extent to which European social policies succeed in escaping from the market's grip and turn towards general issues of gender and generational equity and justice. This market dominance also constitutes the main impediment facing those wishing to revise the existing 'gender order', a term which alludes to the traditions, norms and principles that underlie the allocation of tasks, rights and life perspectives to the two genders over the life course. The term 'order' implies a structure with vertical and horizontal elements. Paid work and unpaid caring do not exist separately, but within a complex system of subordination and precedence.

Women's concerns have to be translated into their own employment issues and into those of their husbands, on whom many still rely. There is, however, a second - perhaps even more important - translating process. The EC member states differ significantly as regards their specific, culture-bound 'gender order'. They diverge in the extent to which women are already a 'natural' part of the workforce, regardless of their domestic circumstances. In some countries social policy is targeted at the working family, in others it supports the concept of a main breadwinner and his (her?) household, and in yet others it relies on all individuals being equally bound to make their own living. In many cases we find a mix of these possibilities. The gender order, as part of a nation's culture, constitutes the frame of reference for the above mentioned translating process. This frame comes into play whenever a member state is asked to adopt EC social policy directives and to transform its laws accordingly. In order to assess the possible outcomes of EC policies at the national level, as well as to understand why women in some countries show little interest in the EC or even some hostility towards further integration, one has to 'gender' the national welfare regimes. This is a task beyond the scope of this paper.

EC social policy, up to now, has strongly focused on market-related social issues like workers' health and safety, social provisions, wages, and the movement of workers (Brewster and Teague, 1989, pp.298). However, economic measures have social effects and social policies can influence the success or otherwise of economic policies. Market transactions as well as social or economic policies may affect women's opportunities, positively or negatively (Keithley, 1991, p.74). The female part of the workforce has already profited immensely from European integration and will continue to do so whenever women succeed in translating their concerns into workers' rights, especially into rights to procedural equality and gender equity within the market. The European Court has turned out to be a woman's ally by improving her employment status. This, in turn, will improve her economic situation in old age.

The next section will focus mainly on Germany. Firstly, the social construction of 'old age' which followed from social security programs is considered. Originally thought of as a means of compensating for income loss in old age (Kolb, 1984), the pension system has created old age as the 'golden years beyond work and duty' (Göckenjan, 1993). This in turn, has changed intergenerational solidarity. It has become more abstract. Some speak of a new antagonism between the young and the old. The main principles of EC policies support the idea of a worker's right to a minimum pension which relieves him or her from work after retirement. It is necessary to consider the extent to which the idea of 'work free' old age, supported by a decent pension, corresponds with women's lives. Freed from what kind of work? EC countries have developed different 'care regimes'. The final part of this essay briefly examines the interface of gender and generational solidarity in various 'caring regimes' and the kinds of burden they involve.

The Social Construction of Old Age Freed From Paid Work

People age, but ageing has many faces. There has been a loosening of formerly strict expectations as to how an elderly person - especially a woman - should live, dress, and move. While pursuing different lifestyles, which are no longer strictly age-bound, people have successfully fought against the supposedly inevitable losses connected with getting older. Paradoxically, social policies, in facilitating a new stage of life open to numerous individual definitions, have created old age in a way it never before existed. They have institutionalised the status passage from work into leisure, from wages to pensions. Thereby, old age has become synonymous with retirement.

The ideas of *ein arbeitsfreies Alter* (old age freed of breadwinning) and of *Ruhestand* (retirement) are relatively new ones, coming into being in the second half of this century in the case of Germany and France. Germany was first in introducing social insurance covering old age (1889), Denmark second (1891) and France third (1895), with Finland as one of the latecomers (1957) due to its belated industrialisation. Germany was again first in including dependants, be they the wife or the children of the deceased worker: during the 1870s for a civil servant's dependants, in 1911 for those of a blue collar worker. However, only the civil servant's pension was high enough to cover living costs; the same was true for the derived pension of his widow. Neither the average blue collar worker, nor - even less - his widow could live on the basis of the scant pension, assuming he or she lived long enough to be able to claim it.

A closer look reveals that, originally, old age benefits had been meant to compensate for income loss due to increasing inability to work. They followed the principles underlying invalidity insurance and were similarly built on the expectation that everyone of the lower social strata worked throughout his or her life, while he or she was 'morally' embedded in a net of mutual obligations. Up to 1957, when West German pensions were reformed, old age benefits were intended as a supplement to other incomes, whether from casual work, household production or savings. Unlike nowadays, old age did not immediately coincide with retiring from paid work. Because social insurance served only as a safety net, it did not constitute a status passage; the more remarkable status changes happened within the life course.

The norm of lifelong work holds true for the British case, too, despite many differences (Ritter, 1983; Hennock, 1987). British insurance was part of the politics of poverty. It was designed to guarantee the deserving, working citizen-voter a status above the non-citizen class when income was lost for reasons over which he - and occasionally she - had no control (Hennock, 1987, p.185). British workers contributed to the pension scheme equally with their employers. The contributions were smaller than those in Germany and they gave entitlement after fewer years; associated with this, all were entitled to the same flat-rate benefits. The German worker's contribution to the old age insurance scheme was income-related; the level of the pension varied substantially in relation to the number of years and the amount of contributions; it made it possible for some elderly workers to retire totally from paid work (ibid.). One can argue, therefore, that the British system had a harsher, universal expectation that everyone would continue to be in paid work (Hockerts, 1982, p.345). On the other hand, as will be shown, the German system particularly disadvantaged working-class women or, more generally, those who did not have continuous work careers, good jobs and high enough wages to contribute to the scheme.

According to Göckenjan (1993, p.8) and Kolb (1984), the norm of self-help and lifelong work underlying old age insurance had been slowly weakening during the earlier part of the twentieth century, due to demographic changes, transformations of the 'traditional' household and labour market contingencies. It was still commonly assumed that work should and could prevent poverty in old age; that the 'sprightly aged are in work' and want to work (Göckenjan, 1993, p.9). However the persistent economic crisis during the years of the Weimar Republic strengthened the idea of decent pensions as a justifiable means to restrict the 'right to work' of able, elderly men. This idea was to some extent realised during the Nazi era.

The 1957 pension reform in West Germany (FRG) turned the hitherto prevailing principles on their head. 'Old age' became a function of the worker's average 40 to 45 working years; that is, of a successful and continuous work career. The latter justified retirement from paid work and a dignified old age on the basis of pensions which by themselves were to guarantee the maintenance of former status and living standards; moreover the pensioner was to profit from subsequent wage rises, the pension therefore being 'dynamic'. The living standards of the worker were treated like property which should be safeguarded after retirement. Nell-Breuning, a Catholic social reformer, influenced the 1957 reform by arguing against any means testing, on the grounds that it would have unfairly attacked the worker's property.

Britain caught up in 1959, by adding an income-related pension to the scant, flat-rate, subsistence pension. France followed in 1970. Taken together, these reforms paved the way for some to a comfortable life without work, for the first time in the history of capitalism. Christopher Pierson (1991) is therefore right in listing three sets of criteria, which taken together define a mature welfare state:

1. the introduction of social insurance;
2. the extension of citizenship and the de-pauperisation of

public welfare (social security as a right, a public duty and a central part of full citizenship, not as charity and benevolence - 'bienfaisance');
3. the growth and level of social expenditure as a whole and of individual benefits.

In the FRG, the pension reforms freed much (male) old age from poverty. Breadwinners could retire to lives given a new meaning, beyond want. Göckenjan and many others stress the extent to which older people have become accustomed to this new stage in their life and have shaped it according to their own needs. A decent life after retirement has become a citizenship right of all those in paid work - including women. An abstract concept of solidarity underlies the social insurance system: that of contributors and - to some extent - taxpayers, who are predominantly employed people, paying for the pensions received by those no longer in paid employment.

Pension systems are now under pressure. The norm of life-long working is mentioned once again, a step-by-step form of retirement discussed and 'just rewards' set against need. A new antagonism between the young and the old is said to have emerged, reminiscent of the traditional one which in former times was often settled by detailed contracts. Studies of demographic changes seem to be implicitly fuelled by a common assumption that the wealth and well-being of the old are financed by the deprivation of the young and, especially, of the middle-aged. It is argued that the latter have to care and pay both ways. Frail, elderly women in particular, outliving their husbands and unable to work and care for themselves or others, are talked of as a 'burden' and in terms of costs. This necessitates a closer, if brief, consideration of how women have fared in the history of socially (and politically) constructed 'workfree' old age.

Old Age As Retirement - From What and For Whom?

Feminist research shows that 'old age beyond work' - beyond earning one's own living - became first and foremost a male standard of normality, in Germany and in other European countries. A woman's daily work never ends, if unpaid caring is taken into account. I will come back to this point later.

Retirement pre-supposes employment. Not all types of work were counted as employment: neither unpaid domestic chores nor caring nor, in some circumstances, farming. Many working women were thus not in employment. Historically, German civil servants' wives did not work, because a civil servant's status did not tolerate a working wife. According to unwritten rules, until recently, a civil servant had been expected to marry; marriage was seen as means of protecting him from the many lures of unmarried life. However, a marriage bar existed for female civil servants. In turn, male civil servants and their households have been generously provided for by the state 'patron'. This provision extended beyond the death of the male breadwinner, granting civil servants' widows unconditionally generous pensions. They had not worked while married, therefore they were not expected to work after the husband's death. State alimony replaced his income. Unsurprisingly, civil servants' widows have always constituted an affluent group amongst solo women. A similar assumption - housewifery - regulated the pension claims of the white collar employee's widow. Benefits depended solely on proving a 30 per cent inability to work and German state-corporatist society did not force her to take any job; like other women from the upper strata, neither was she expected to do the housework by herself. These general assumptions of a husband's and a wife's differing proper place and duty also shaped old age policies in other countries, despite differences in detail.

The majority of working class women, however, worked and were expected to work. Many working women - many more than men - failed to contribute to the insurance schemes because they worked intermittently and/or they earned wages too small to contribute. Therefore, only a few women, far fewer than men, profited in 1916 when the retirement age was reduced from age 70 to 65. In addition, only the frail working class widow could claim a widow's pension, through proving a more than 50 per cent inability to work. It was generally assumed that married working class women worked, that they relied to a lesser or marginal extent on a male breadwinner and that, therefore, the breadwinner's death was a minor risk for them compared with that for the upper class housewife. Assumptions like these explain why turn-of-the-century feminists never picked up the issue of old age pensions but rather concentrated on health and safety issues; they further explain why working class widows could claim only a percentage of the husband's pension. In contemporary Germany, this ratio amounts to 60 per cent for widows of all social classes (Ellerkamp, 1985; 1992).

In most EC countries, pensions are related both to income and to working years. Low paid workers' widows therefore risk poverty even when they have been hard-working wives. Poverty in old age has always been and still is a women's issue, despite some improvement due to women's increased labour market participation, higher qualifications and improved wages.

Social policies in most EC countries have been gender-biased in many ways. Women have been expected to earn their own living and to care for children and a husband. They have been fully or partly freed from paid work whenever this was thought necessary for the well-being of others: e.g. to help the male civil servant to live up to his status, to take care of small children and a busy husband; or, later in life, to care for parents and parents in-law. Promulgating his social security plans, Bismarck presented the male worker's pension as an opportunity for the wife to take care of her father-in-law! Contemporary, empirical evidence suggests that a woman 'naturally' retires, at the same time as her husbands, for his sake, thereby risking a lower pensions. Women have been blamed for working and taking away jobs from men whenever there has been a crisis in the labour market. In turn, women have preferred welfare mixes that enabled them to be both carers and workers to 'either-or' solutions or full-time double burdens. As a result they have had to rely, at least partly, on the male breadwinner's income and, after his death, on widows' pensions. In fact, in some EC countries, the majority of women receive widows' pensions significantly higher than those earned by their own contributions. Women's well-being and freedom from paid work during the life course have depended on the breadwinner-husband, his continuous work career and a stable marriage.

The bonds of marriage are loosening and, consequently, the pattern of male breadwinning is being eroded. Kathleen Gerson (1991) argues that these changes have affected women and men differently, with women facing the greater burden.

Some social arrangements have changed significantly, but not all. Most households now depend on wives' and mothers' income; nevertheless, most women remain segregated in relatively ill-rewarded jobs and responsible 'for the lion's share of household labour' (ibid., p. 36). Men's ability and commitment to support of wives and children have reduced, but most men still enjoy significant economic and social advantages (ibid., p. 37). Gerson speaks of men's 'conflict between preserving their historic privileges and confronting their growing need to share breadwinning responsibilities with women' (ibid.). In many countries, this conflict seems to be solved at the expense of the majority of women of all ages.

Most women are, at least for some time, carers. However, a norm that allows retirement from caring, akin to the retirement from paid work, has never existed for women. Janet Finch and Jennifer Mason (1993) found persisting moral guidelines that define the few exceptions for women from expectations that they will care for their kin. Unsurprisingly, widowhood means, for many women, retirement from taking care of the husband. In contrast to lone elderly men, most women - including those who do not get a generous widow's pension - 'find rewards in solo living and prefer it to living in the home of their adult children' (ibid. p.177).

EC social policies focus on employment. They guarantee some social rights for those who are employed or ready to enter employment. On the face of it, EC equal opportunity policies seem to advantage lone - independent and mobile - women. Jane Millar (1990), however, argues that solo women do not differ much from other women in that most of them will care for somebody else in their family during their life course. In her view, 'women are sometimes solo and sometimes married, sometimes they have caring responsibilities and sometimes they do not. But the times when they do have caring responsibilities - whether they are solo or married - carry heavy costs, both in the short and long term'. All modern societies rely on women as paid and - still more - as unpaid carers. She argues, therefore, that policies which focus on the needs of women as wives and mothers are also the right way to promote equality for solo women. The EC is far from taking this point of view. 'Woman-friendly' policies in a market economy would be close to 'squaring a circle': granting women an equal right to work and the choice of how to care. Those kinds of policies have yet to be invented. So far, the EC is a community of full-time working males and of 'their' families.

'Caring Regimes', Gender and Obligations

It is thus clear that social policies assume a fully 'commodified', full-time and continuously working individual. Social security schemes grant 'exit options' and help to avoid exploitable dependencies. They 'decommodify' those who were fully commodified. Feminists argue that unpaid services provided by mothers and wives contribute to (mostly) the man's continuous work career, to his commodification, while decreasing women's labour market chances and bargaining power.

Welfare regimes, however, differ as regards the extent to which they are built on the premise of unpaid or poorly paid services. In what follows, culture-bound 'care regimes' are considered from the bottom-up point of view of those in need of care (see Jamieson, 1991).

'Culture' alludes to a body of shared understandings within a particular society. These define who is expected to provide care, for whom, in what ways, and whether the state, the market or the family is the primary or the secondary provider of care according to more or less institutionalized rules of reciprocity.

Janet Finch and Jennifer Mason (1993) describe the diversity of attitudes towards family responsibilities. They stress the difference between moral obligations that are forced upon members of societies and moral guidelines which people use in order to decide - in a specific context - whether they are responsible for care and how that care should be provided, e.g. in cash or in kind. Moral obligations and moral guidelines are therefore shifting and contingent resources for policy makers.

Shared understandings and common cultural points of reference can be argued to constitute the identity of a nation. They resist major changes and can often re-emerge as 'old wine in new bottles' in processes of social change. What is meant by shared understandings? Let us consider some examples.

The third page of Adalbert Ever's and Thomas Olk's report on care for the frail elderly in Germany (1991, p.61) includes a diagram on the 'shrinking potential for care by daughters:

women between the ages of 45-59' due to demographic changes. Fertility has steadily declined in all western societies. But only in the FRG was it publicly talked of in terms of a 'shrinking potential for care by daughters' and as a severe challenge to our welfare regime that necessitated immediate action. A report on Denmark, on the UK, or even on pronatalist France would take another starting point.

There are cultural differences in dealing with population issues like fertility rates: the FRG as well as the GDR, France, Greece and, some decades ago, Sweden and Denmark worried about their population decline - but never the UK. Some countries developed overtly pro-natalist policies, others more indirect ones. Population policy regimes followed various patterns: that of no choice and no support; that of private choice (no state intervention into family affairs) and no support (or minimal support as in the UK, in order to prevent children's poverty); private choice and public support (as in the Nordic countries); no or little choice and public support.

The principle of subsidiarity prevails in Christian Democratic care regimes, such as in Germany. Subsidiarity can be best explained by asking: If there is a social problem - a child or another family member in need of care - who should be the primary source of care? Following the principle, the answer would be those closest to the person or problem in question. In the case of the child, this would be first the mother, then the immediate family, followed by other kin, and so on. Any intervention by those less close to the problem has to be justified. It is assumed that a 'differential pull' (Hoff Sommers, 1992) exists - in contrast to the 'equal pull' underlying the idea of a general, revenue-based, universal service-state. People feel 'differentially pulled' into caring duties, depending on whether the person in need is a relative or someone less 'familiar'. The strength of social and moral obligations depends on the relationship of the care-giver to the care recipient; this in turn depends on culturally transmitted norms and rules which allocate problems and their solutions - obligations to care - within a hierarchical social order. The state, that is the wider community, is allowed to support the mother, for example, by money transfers and other policies in order to promote the particular quality of the mother-child relationship.

German family policy - before and after the Nazi era - saw

the family, with its differential roles and statuses, as the foundation of and model for the wider society. It was believed that this 'traditionally modern' family would buttress social order; the argument being similar to that put forward by functionalist sociologists, such as Talcott Parsons, and by some communitarians like Michael Walzer. In fact, this model of family life can be traced back to Aristotle, one of the ideological fathers of Catholicism, with his functionalist foundation of separate roles for women and men, and the assertion of women's natural subordination for the sake of the whole. If there are natural differences between women and men, the community should provide the means by which these can develop and flourish. Family policies should thus help women to become 'women', with different obligations and occupations from those of men; and men should be enabled to become 'men' heads of households, breadwinners, gatekeepers of the boundaries between the private-domestic and the public spheres.

The French systems of care rely on similiar principles. As in Germany, the policy focus is on institutions, such as the family or the work relationship, rather than on individuals. Strong family policies are based on the idea of citizens' solidarity, arising from the debt which they owe to the community in which they are raised. They are designed to help larger families (i.e. with more than two children) to maintain a decent standard of living. However, whereas Germany employs 'family policy' as a kind of 'negative labour market policy' - discouraging women's labour market participation and encouraging them to spend periods of their lives being solely a mother and wife - France supports both. Women's work, paid and unpaid, is seen as their natural contribution to the family's welfare and to motherhood.

What about the Nordic countries; how do they answer the question 'who is the primary provider of care'? The state, financed by the taxpayer, is the response. The Nordic model can be described as a state-enhanced, female service economy: women help women to be employed by providing paid care. Therefore, Hoff Sommers' 'equal pull' principle does not properly describe the Nordic welfare regime, despite the assumptions in Esping-Andersen's writings (1990). Esping-Andersen stresses the extent to which social rights in Scandinavian societies are based on the principle of equality.

However, it is solely women who are 'pulled' into caring jobs and obligations, not men. Nevertheless, unlike the situation in Germany and France, the offspring are not expected to be the main carers for their parents, nor are the parents - mainly mothers - expected to be the predominant carers for their children.

Despite the strength of family ties, the Nordic model is not built on continuous caring relationships between the young and the old; instead, these relationships take 'the form of general socializing and occasional help' (Jamieson 1991, p. 118). It is the state, county and municipality which provide health and social services free: funded by taxes, a universal citizen's right and based on the employment of women as carers. The right to services, in turn, is inextricably linked to being or having been in paid work.

On the face of it, individualization seems to have developed to its full potential in the Nordic welfare regimes: individual taxation, no or very small widows' pensions, a freedom to live in a variety of family forms, and so on. However, the Nordic societies, especially Finland, can be argued to resemble traditional, extended households with kin or 'trust' based relations. The traditional household expected each member to work for her or his living and to take care of her/himself. This was true for children and the aged as much as for others. The household economy was built on everyone's lifelong work and care. In Scandinavian societies, the state has replaced the household. However, the norm of lifelong work underlies social rights. Everyone has to be a worker citizen in order to be entitled to support.

Anne Jamieson (1991) compares two contrasting care regimes: West Germany and Denmark. She compares her results with the British situation.

In the FRG, an elderly frail person in need is normally cared for - in more than 90 per cent of cases - by a close relative: most frequently, a wife or husband; then a daughter or daughter-in-law, and so on. Most men die while married. Therefore, it is mainly elderly frail women who are in need of care from other than their spouse. To obtain this care, it is necessary to be defined - via a doctor - as ill, preferably as 'curably' ill. The care is then paid for by a woman's health insurance. A strict divide exists between illness-related care paid for by health insurance - the better provision - and publicly provided social services which must be paid for by the individual herself or, if she is poor, by welfare agencies. If illness develops into chronic disability, the health insurance ceases to pay. Any help at home or residential care has to be paid for. Women (the majority) who cannot pay themselves either have to claim means-tested welfare benefits and/or seek financial support from their children. Children are forced by law to support their parents in need. Many women of the middle generation leave the labour market in order to care for a frail mother. In some, when private or charitable resources prove inadequate, 'much of the burden rests on the family' (ibid.). The principle is quite explicit and widely accepted: the family has a duty to look after older relatives. In practice, this means that women in particular suffer a great deal of stress and deprivation in an attempt to care for relatives.

Denmark, in contrast, has started from the agrarian tradition that nobody should be another's burden - be it a child or an elderly person. The offspring are not expected to care. This tradition was strengthened by labour shortage during the 1970s and the pressure to relieve women from caring responsibilities at home. Most elderly people in need of care now live in publicly funded institutions. The principle of universalism dominates health as well as social services (100 per cent state dominance in provision; universal rights rather than contribution-based rights). In Denmark, more money is spent on personal social services than on health care. A new focus on home-based care has developed recently. In 1988, the divide between care in residential or nursing homes and home care was abolished. Older people in need of care now have the same rights to services regardless of how and where they live; they do not have to leave their familiar home and neighbourhood. Instead of new nursing homes, dwellings 'suitable for older people' are built. Every unit must have its own bathroom and kitchen facilities. Thereby, older people are enabled to live independently as far as possible (ibid.). They will never have to give up more autonomy than is strictly necessary.

The impetus behind the new legislation is undeniably the desire to reduce costly, institutional care. But it derives from shared understandings of old age. Policies are based on the principle of enhancing the independence of older people. Therefore, contrary to trends in the FRG or the UK, 'home help is still widely provided to a large proportion of older people, and there is as yet very little debate about concentrating services mainly on those who might otherwise need institutional or hospital care' (ibid.). Unsurprisingly, neither family members nor other kinds of informal carers play a major role on the policy agenda.

Outlook

Germany and Denmark reveal different welfare traditions; and they give insights into some barriers to change. The dominance of the insurance principle in health care, and the dominance of the principle of continuous labour market participation which is embedded into the logic of insurance - not to speak of the vested interests of labour market partners - are structures highly resistant to any change.

The Nordic countries are said to be on the move from a service state towards a social insurance state. Up to the present, however, nothing indicates that they will expect 'filial morality' (Hoff Sommers, 1992): the mutual obligation of the young and the old to care. Solidarity has remained that of the taxpayer for his or her community. Instead, incentives are offered to those who do keep their kin at home - with little regard as to whether they still undertake paid work - and incentives are also offered to those older people who remain in their homes and rely on domiciliary help. A duty to care cannot be forced upon the family - and neither can women be forced to retreat fully from the labour market and be dependent on a male breadwinner in societies which have not developed such a norm. However, the care allowances will be cut back. This may lead in time to new relationships between the two genders and between the generations.

Jamieson argues that the role of the family is less clear in the UK than in Germany or in Denmark. Implicit or tacit expectations exist. The UK is moving from a service state, albeit one with low levels of provision, to a market 'buy out' of social services. A hierarchy is emerging: from needs for care which are clearly marketable, to those which necessitate the 24 hour presence of what Clare Ungerson (1992) calls 'quasi-kin' doing 'quasi-work'. By this, she means badly paid carers who take the money as top-up payments to Income Support or Invalid Care Allowance. The vulnerable care for the vulnerable. Women care for women. What has happened to the idea of protecting the vulnerable people from 'exploitable dependencies' which used to be at the core of welfare (Goodin 1988)?

References

Arber, S. and Ginn, J. (1991) *Gender and Later Life*. London: Sage.

Brewster, C. and Teague, P. (1989) *European Community Social Policy. Its Impact on the UK*.London Institute of Personnel Management.

Ellerkamp, M. (1985) 'Witwenversorgung 1850-1912. Zur Geschichte der Unterprivilegierung von Frauen in der Sozialpolitik', in Forschungsschwerpunkt Reproduktionsrisiken, soziale Bewegungen und Sozialpolitik (ed.) *Sozialpolitik und Sozialstaat*. Bericht zum 10 Oktober , Teil 1, Universität Bremen pp.289-342.

Ellerkamp, M. (1992) 'Witwenrente' in Bauer, R. (ed.) *Lexikon des Sozial- und Gesundheitswesens*, München, pp.2165-2168.

Esping-Andersen, G. (1990) *The Three Worlds of Welfare Capitalism*. Cambridge: Polity.

Evers, A. and Olk, T. (1991) 'The mix of care provisions for the frail elderly in the Federal Republic of Germany' in Evers, A. und Svetlik, I. (eds.) *New Welfare Mixes in Care for the Elderly*. Eurosocial, Reports 40, Vol. 1, Vienna, pp.59-100.

Finch, J. and Mason, J. (1993)*Negotiating Family Responsibilities*. London: Tavistock/Routledge.

Gerson, K. (1991) 'Coping with commitment: dilemmas and conflicts of family life' in Wolfe, A. (ed.) *America at Century's End,* Berkeley: University of Berkeley Press.

Göckenjan, G. (1993): 'Alter - Ruhestand - Generationsvertrag? Zum Altersdiskurs aus historisch-struktureller Perspektive', *Aus Politik und Zeitgeschichte*, B 17/93, April, pp.3-10.

Goodin, R.E. (1988) *Reasons For Welfare. The Political Theory of the Welfare State*. Princeton: Princeton University Press.

Hennock, A.P. (1987) *British Social Reforms and German Precedents. The Case of Social Insurance 1880-1914*. Oxford: Clarendon Press.

Hockerts, H.G. (1982) 'Deutsche Nachkriegssozialpolitik vor dem Hintergrund des Beveridge-Plans' in Mommsen, W.J. (ed.) *Die Entstehung des Wohlfahrtsstaates in Großbritannien und Deutschland 1850-1950*. Stuttgart: Klett-Cotta.

Hoff Sommers, C. (1992) 'Filiale Moralität' in Nunner-Winkler, G. (ed.) *Weibliche Moral. Die Kontroverse um eine geschlechtsspezifische Ethik*. Frankfurt: Campus.

Jamieson, A. (1991) 'Community care for older people: policies in Britain, West Germany and Denmark' in Room, G. (ed.) *Towards A European Welfare State?* Bristol: SAUS, pp.107-126.

Keithley, J. (1991) 'Social security in a single market', in Room, G. (ed.) *Towards A European Welfare State?* Bristol: SAUS.

Kolb, R. (1984) 'Hinterbliebenenversicherung oder Hinterbliebenenversorgung' in *Deutsche Rentenversicherung*, 11, pp.635-649.

Millar, J. (1990) 'The socio-economic situation of single women in Europe' in O'Brien, M. et al. (eds.) *Women, Equal Opportunities and Welfare*. Cross-National Research Papers, New Series, No. 3. Birmingham: Aston University, pp.29-42.

Pierson, C. (1991) *Beyond the Welfare State? The New Political Economy of Welfare*. Cambridge: Polity Press.

Raasch, S. (1990) 'Gleichberechtigung im EG-Binnenmarkt' in *Kritische Justiz*, 23(1), pp.62-78.

Ritter, G.A. (1983) *Sozialversicherung in Deutschland und England. Entstehung und Grundzüge im Vergleich*. München: Beck.

Ungerson, C. (1992) 'Payment for caring - mapping a territory'. Paper for the Social Policy Association Annual Conference, July, University of Nottingham.

Understanding old age: social and policy issues

CHRIS PHILLIPSON

Introduction

The impact of an ageing population has given rise to considerable debate and discussion over the past few years. These discussions have emerged against a background of rapid change in terms of the context of ageing: first, the growth in public awareness and interest in ageing issues - these sharpened to some degree by the European year of older people and solidarity between generations (Age Concern, 1992); second, the impact of legislation in the field of community care and the movement towards a mixed economy of care (Phillipson, 1992); third, the growth in early retirement and the evolving concept of 'the third age', this raising issues about changes in policies and attitudes to realise the full potential of this period (Midwinter, 1992).

The purpose of this chapter is to review - from a sociological perspective - some of the issues which will need to be tackled in these debates; to identify recent developments in the field of social gerontology; and, finally, to indicate agendas for future research in the field of ageing studies.

The Sociology of Old Age

An initial observation is that the sociology of old age remains an undeveloped area in the UK. Despite the remarkable work of Peter Townsend in the 1950s and 1960s - and both the *Family Life of Old People* and *The Last Refuge* are surely classic works of sociology of this period - the subsequent record has been a disappointing one. Certainly, in terms of the growth period of sociology, during the late 1960s and through to the early 1980s, work in the sociology of old age was somewhat limited in terms of its theoretical content and empirical ambitions - an issue explored by this author, along with Graham Fennell and Helen Evers, in *The Sociology of Old Age*. In part, this was because of the strength of another tradition of enquiry - social policy and social administration. In this area, studies of, or including, older people have been firmly established in a line from Booth, Rowntree, Beveridge, Titmuss, Townsend and Wedderburn. This tradition has been enormously creative both in terms of establishing the extent of poverty experienced by older people, and influencing Government policy in areas such as pension reform, social security, and health and social policy (Walker, 1981).

Despite the importance and value of approaches drawn from social policy and social administration, the urgent need for new perspectives on old age were being highlighted from the late 1970s. The reasons for this are both general and more specific to the period under discussion. In terms of the former, a sociology of old age provides a different and necessary perspective about the issues facing older people. The sociologist starts from the view that old age is interesting because - although it is an enduring human phenomenon handled differently by different societies - it is changing and influencing social behaviour. The sociologist is concerned to explore the processes involved and how they are being interpreted by men and women. This approach contrasts with social policy and government interests in old age. In these contexts, old age is regarded as a problem (for the economy or the health service, for instance), hence the need for some analysis and collection of data. This approach has its own validity and justification but it leads to a distorted view of older people, together with a limited selection of topics to be analysed and discussed. It leads, in addition, to a focus on the weaknesses of older people, rather than on their strengths, together with an emphasis on their similarities rather than their differences (Fennell et al., 1988).

Sociological perspectives have an additional, general contribution to make, namely, clarifying the nature of long - term social trends. The emergence of retirement is one example. This can be viewed as an economic problem - for the individual and for society - or as a psychological issue leading to problems of adjustment (Phillipson, 1993). However, retirement may also be seen as creating major changes in social relationships and activities. Earlier retirement, for example, is leading to a re-evaluation of the balance between work and leisure, with a greater emphasis on constructing a lifestyle which either combines elements of paid work with longer periods of leisure and continuing education, or which focuses exclusively on recreational pursuits (Schuller and Bostyn, 1992).

These developments raise many important questions: will this trend stimulate yet further expansion in the service sector of the economy; who will gain and who will lose as the period of time spent in full-time work contracts; what are the implications for the family; will patterns of care change or remain the same as the work/leisure balance is changed; will the household division of labour be modified with some older men taking on a broader range of domestic and caring responsibilities? (Laczko and Phillipson, 1991).

None of the above questions can be answered in the absence of a sociological perspective. Indeed, the fact that they await answers (and are the subject of much confusion in policy circles) reflects the current weaknesses in the sociology of old age.

The above points are reinforced by the nature of the debate about old age in the 1980s and early 1990s. Here, there are two main points to consider: first, the fiscal crisis in the welfare state has placed older people in the spotlight as the main beneficiaries of public expenditure (Longman, 1987; Johnson et al., 1989; Phillipson, 1990). This has given rise to questions such as: are we spending too much on the old? Are we in danger of depriving the young of resources? Are taxes (to pay for items such as pensions and social security) sapping the motivations of workers and entrepreneurs? Such questions began to be asked in the 1970s and continued with a vengeance under Thatcherite social policy in the 1980s. Second, there was belated recognition in the 1980s of the extent of demographic change. Despite the 1949 Royal Commission on Population and the 1954 Phillips Report (whose estimate of a population of 9.5 million over pensionable age by 1979 was accurate to within a few thousand elders), Governments expressed surprise in the late 70s and early 80s at the extent of population ageing. This was used as a justification for curtailing public expenditure in general and spending on older people in particular (Bornat et al., 1985).

On the one side, then, has been increasing concern about

the financing of the welfare state; on the other side, increased awareness about the extent of the demographic shift which has taken place over the post-war period. Both these developments have gone some way to re-awaken an interest on the part of social scientists about issues relating to old age. In particular, there has been a lively debate over the past 10 years focusing on the theme of the political economy of old age. The political economy perspective grew out of the politicisation of issues surrounding old age, together with the problems faced by traditional theories in developing an effective response to the unfolding crisis in public expenditure. Some of the key studies using this perspective have included: *The Aging Enterprise* by Carroll Estes (1979); 'The structured dependency of the elderly' by Peter Townsend (1981); 'Towards a political economy of old age' by Alan Walker (1981); *Political Economy, Health and Aging* by Estes, Gerard, Zones and Swan (1984); *Old Age in the Welfare State* by John Myles (1984), and *Ageing and Social Policy* edited by Chris Phillipson and Alan Walker (1986). A general review of this approach has been brought together in a collection edited by Minkler and Estes (1991) entitled *Critical Perspectives on Aging*. Some of the main themes of this approach will now be discussed and some issues identified for future research.

The Rise of Critical Gerontology

A major concern of the above studies was to challenge a view of growing old as a period dominated by physical and mental decline (the biomedical model of aging). This model was attacked for its association of age with disease, as well as for the way that it individualised and medicalised the ageing process. The approach taken by what may be termed critical gerontology, is a view that old age is a social rather than a biologically constructed status. In the light of this, many of the experiences affecting older people can be seen as a product of a particular division of labour and structure of inequality, rather than a natural part of the ageing process. Alan Walker (1981) elaborated this perspective with his concept of the 'social creation of dependency' in old age, and Peter Townsend (1981) used a similar term when he described the 'structured dependency' of older people. This dependency was seen to be the consequence of the forced exclusion of older people from work, the experience of poverty, institutionalisation and restricted domestic and community roles. Finally, Carroll Estes introduced the term the 'aging enterprise':

> ...to call particular attention to how the aged are often processed and treated as a commodity in our society and to the fact that the age-segregated policies that fuel the ageing enterprise are socially-divisive "solutions" that single-out, stigmatise, and isolate the aged from the rest of society (Estes, 1979, p.2)

The paradigm developed by the political economy approach is shared by developments in the study of other age groups. For example, many of the themes in the collection of essays edited by James and Prout (1991) *Constructing and Reconstructing Childhood,* explore issues debated in social gerontology in the 1980s. The connections between age groups have been further explored by Hockey and James (1993) *Growing Up and Growing Old.* A central theme of this study is the extent to which power is lost and gained at different points through the life course, and the possibility of both young and older people being affected by processes of infantalisation.

In respect of the social construction or political economy of old age the main themes of this approach have been concerned with:

1   Challenging a form of biological reductionism, whereby the real physiological and biological changes which take place with ageing are often used as a justification for denying old people the right to participate in decisions which affect them and generally to limit the extent to which they control their lives.

2   Showing that age must be seen in relation to the individual's location within the social structure, including factors such as: race, class, gender, and the type of work (paid and unpaid) performed by an individual through his or her life.

3.   Demonstrating that later life is a time of reconstruction, with older people active in the search for meaning - through work, leisure and intimate friendships.

4. That the lives of older people are in tension with the nature of capitalism as an economic and social system, with the poverty of older people, their exclusion from work and their image as a burden on society, reflecting this tension (Phillipson, 1982; Phillipson, 1991).

The political economy model has certainly been fruitful in terms of the analysis of ageing at macro-economic and macro-social levels, with important studies in relation to areas such as work and retirement, the fiscal crisis of welfare, and the structural causes of ageism. However, there has been less success in understanding the daily lives of older people and the extent to which these are being re-shaped by the changing attitudes of elderly people themselves. Certainly, we do have an increasing number of studies exploring the social relations of older people: Wenger's (1984) *The Supportive Network,* Walker and Qureshi's (1989) *The Caring Relationship*, Bury and Holmes's (1992) *Life After Ninety*, and Jerrome's (1993) *Good Company* are relevant examples. But it also clear that we need new types of studies if we are to give a convincing picture of the daily life of people in the third and fourth age (Thompson et al's (1989) *I Don't Feel Old* is one of the few to explore this area in any detail). In terms of the kind of research which will be needed, four areas will be briefly reviewed:

- intimacy and sexuality in old age;
- studying late old age;
- relationships between kin;
- relationships between generations.

Intimacy and Sexuality in Old Age

A perhaps surprising fact in terms of understanding the lives of older people is that we know very little about patterns of intimacy and sexuality in old age. The work of Dorothy Jerrome (1993) has been important in revealing details of the friendships formed by older people, although more work on this topic, using different types of samples and from contrasting communities, is certainly necessary. A major aspect of intimate relations is still, however, largely unresearched in the British context, namely, relationships between spouses. Most studies take the marriages or the long-term relationship within homosexual or lesbian households for granted, the major focus usually being on the nature of informal care - who provides it and under what conditions. Alternatively, studies have been concerned with understanding the lives of older people once a partner has died (Bowling and Cartwright, 1982). Yet it is worth considering the fact that because of longevity, far from marriage being in decline, a higher proportion of people are married today than in Victorian times: in 1991 (figures for 1891 in brackets), of people aged 60-64, 81 per cent were married (74 per cent); of those 65-69, the proportion was 79 per cent (69 per cent); of those 70-74, it was 76 per cent (59 per cent); of those 75-79, it was 69 per cent (49 per cent); of those 80-84, it was 59 per cent (39 per cent); and of those over 85, it was 43 per cent (28 per cent).

The significance of these changes is reinforced by earlier retirement and changes in household composition. The former has meant an increase in the amount of time couples can choose to spend with each other, ahead of some of the health changes associated with late old age. The latter is illustrated by the decline of co-residence between elderly parents and their adult children, a change which gathered momentum from the 1960s onwards (Wall, 1992). The development of long-term marriages, within the context of earlier retirement and the decline of co-residence with children, represents an important phenomenon which has yet to receive serious investigation. Research is needed to focus upon the various pressures and challenges which may face older couples. Couples within these marriages are exposed to a wide variety of life-changing events and transitions. Later-life transitions have the potential to be experiences of growth and positive change, but they also have the potential for dysfunction and loss. From a sociological and social psychological perspective, it has been argued that couples may not be socialised into handling these transitions, although they are more likely to view marriage as a lifetime commitment governed by normative obligations (Finch, 1989; Szinovacz, Ekerdt and Vinick, 1992). One example here is the pressure on marriages resulting from the need to provide care. Evandrou et al. (1986) demonstrate that over 90 per cent of married elderly people with a disability are helped with domestic and personal self-care tasks by their spouse. In these circumstances the biography of the relationship and the marriage may be crucial in terms of support for the disabled person. Given the pressures associated with community care, research on the social world of older couples would seem a significant priority.

Studying Late Old Age

The second area to be considered concerns the issue of how we study the world of the very elderly, and especially those in their 90s and beyond - a group of increasing importance in society. The need to consider this issue has been underlined by the publication of a book called *Life After Ninety*, by Michael Bury and Anthea Holme (1991). This study reports on the lives of nearly 200 people aged 90 and over, living at home and in communal establishments. It is the first British study of its kind and provides important details about the health, social and personal circumstances of very elderly people. The authors provide valuable data about the lives of their subjects. The reader is inevitably struck by the constraints and barriers faced by the group: the serious deafness faced by more than half; the 59 per cent who never go out; the two-thirds who are unable to prepare a meal; the 50 per cent who are unable to negotiate stairs; and the 12 per cent who cannot wash their face or hands. Yet one is struck even more by the apparent resilience in the face of these troubles: most are never lonely; few feel any sense of boredom; most usually look forward to the day on waking. This is a group of stoics who appear not to complain - at least not to medical sociologists conducting surveys.

And here we come to a central complaint about much of social gerontology thus far - it is all a pretty bloodless affair: it tells us the story we perhaps want to hear: that life after 90 is great: you may be deaf, unable to go out or prepare a meal: but, well, life is not too bad - consider the alternative as they say. But we should perhaps start reviewing how we tell this particular story, consider it in a different way, and ask some different questions. We need to be more critical about questionnaires which fail to relate to the unfolding and changing pattern of people's lives. And we must also explore with greater rigour some practical issues: how do we interview people where impaired hearing is the norm? How does a significant degree of hearing loss change the conduct of the interviews, the quality of interaction, and the relationship between the people involved? Another example: we need to recognise that interviewing a 90 year old (or an 80 year old for that matter) in contrast, say, to a 30 year old, raises different interpretive issues: the 30 year old takes pretty much granted that they have reached 30 and may have a fairly clear idea of what this stage in the life course involves. But is the same true of our 90 year olds? Did they expect to reach this age? How do they make sense of their lives in this period given the (relative) scarcity of, for example, other 90 year olds and the uncertainty surrounding their relationship with other age groups?

Relationships Between Kin

The third area for research concerns that of relationships between kin. Here, it might be argued that lay, government and some academic views, have become stuck in something of a time warp. The conventional wisdom about older people and the family goes something like this:

1. Old people still live close to at least one child.
2. Old people with adult children still see them regularly.
3. Old people who need care want to be cared for by their children.

All of these statements suggest rather complex sociological questions, all of which are in urgent need of investigation. The sociologist (and social gerontologist) should be prepared to dig deep into the privacy of the family to search for those alterations in behaviour which suggest profound changes in values and attitudes. They must, in the words of Paul Theroux (1989) ask 'endless pestering questions' to get at the nature of family life (and the place of older people within it) as the twentieth century draws to a close. In particular, they might be concerned with:

1. Those older people without a child close by -they never had children or children have been geographically mobile.
2. Those children who are not regular visitors - perhaps their visits are enjoyed more or serve different functions than those who do the twice weekly and Sunday lunch - time ritual;
3. Those older people whose preference is not to be cared for by their children.

In general, it seems to me that the debate about intergenerational relations needs to be re-assessed. Research from studies by Patrick West and his colleagues in Scotland (West et al., 1984) and Anne Salvage and her colleagues in Wales (Salvage, 1989) (as well as opinion poll surveys), suggest that the preferences of older and younger adults may be moving away from reliance upon informal care in time of need. This may be especially the case in situations where there is a long-term commitment arising out of a chronic illness (Lee, 1985), or the need to provide personal care (Ungerson, 1987).

The arguments about changing care preferences are highlighted by research on patterns of kinship obligations. Janet Finch (1989), in a major review of work in this area, has highlighted the complex set of rules determining the provision of family care. She notes that kin relationships do not operate on the basis of a ready -made set of moral rules, clearly laid out for older people and their carers to follow. In particular, the 'sense of obligation' which marks the distinctive character of kin relations, does not follow a reliable and consistent path in terms of social practice. Finch writes:

> It is actually much less reliable than that. It is nurtured and grows over time between some individuals more strongly than others, and its practical consequences are highly variable. It does have a binding quality, but that derives from commitments built up between real people over many years, not from an abstract set of moral values (Finch, 1989, p.242).

This argument is important because it cuts across a central thrust of government policy on community care, namely, that families act as though there are cultural and moral scripts which they follow in supporting older people in times of crisis or dependency. Moreover, the argument is taken a stage further by some researchers with the assertion that older people themselves follow this path, with an almost instinctive tendency to move towards the family rather than bureaucratic agencies. According to Wenger:

> Research from a wide cross-section of developed countries demonstrates that not only does most care come from the family ... but that most people think that this is where the responsibility should lie (Wenger, 1984, p.14).

This argument, however, relies upon a historical perspective which may no longer be acceptable as an accurate portrayal of the kind of care wanted by people. Families are variable in their response to requests for help and, in any event, the care given is always negotiated within a social and biographical context (Finch, 1989). The conventional wisdom is still assuming that the family is alive and well and virtually unchanged since Peter Townsend (1957) described it in Bethnal Green in the 1950s. The issue here is in part methodological - we have more studies of the family life of the old but the data is still being collected within a conceptual map which assumes that the family really is all-important and that reliance upon it by the old continues as a sociological fact. This may be the case in some areas and amongst some groups; but the range of experiences and ties of obligation and support is certainly far more diverse some forty years on from the social world of older people in the East End of London.

Relationships Between Generations

A fourth area for sociological analysis concerns the relationship between generations. This issue has arisen from the influence of a political and economic discourse which has emphasised the possible tension between generations arising from an ageing population. This question has, however, been muddled by the elision between economic and sociological generations. In fact, these should really be seen as two distinct entities, each with its own particular dynamic and set of relationships. With the economic generation, issues are presented in terms of discrete groups competing - selfishly or otherwise - for a fair share of resources. At its most extreme, this model suggests that generations behave as if on a collision course, with the block votes of the old threatening to cut off services needed by the young (Longman, 1987), and the young reconsidering the basis of the welfare contract and supporting threats to dismantle the welfare state (Thompson, 1989).

The sociological generation will, however, almost certainly behave in a rather different way. What does the sociologist mean when he or she uses the term 'generation'? Philip Abrams (1982), in his classic essay 'Identity and the problems of generations', used the definition adopted by Rudolf Heberle, namely, that a generation consisted: '... "of contemporaries of approximately the same age" but for whom age is established not by the calendar of years but by a calender of events and experiences'. Heberle concluded that: 'A generation is a phenomenon of collective mentality and morality. [The members] of a generation feel themselves linked by a community of standpoints, of beliefs and wishes' (Abrams, 1982, p.258). But the identification of people as belonging to a particular generation is a complex process. Abrams himself points out that the cut-off points between generations are often obscure and may only develop gradually as part of a long historical process. And this point has been further developed by the American historian Andrew Achenbaum (1986), who suggests that the meaning of the term 'generation' is 'both fuzzy and arbitrary' (Achenbaum 1986, p.93). He argues:

> Less clear cut than the distinction between parent and child, the term may refer with equal plausibility to all people between certain ages, to progenitor of any age (as opposed to their progeny), and/or to people who lived through a monumental experience such as the great Depression). The very ambiguity of meaning makes it hard to know who is precisely included or excluded in such as definition. Worse, referring to people as being of a certain generation attributes to them characteristics which they may or may not possess. Who, after all, is a member of the "gypped generation"? Where and how does one draw the line: on the basis of age? birth order? income? expectations? (Achenbaum 1986, pp.93-94).

This last point is of fundamental importance and was central to the position adopted by Karl Mannheim (1952) in his essay 'The problem of generations'. Contrary to much of the present speculation about the possible behaviour of generations, Mannheim noted that the characteristic of what he termed 'generational units' was that their location and effectiveness in social systems could not be explained adequately on the basis of age alone. Following this, Abrams writes that:

> Age is a necessary but not a sufficient condition for their existence. Other factors such as class, religion, race,

occupation, institutional setting, in short all the conventional categories of socio-structural analysis. In other words, the study of generations brings to light consequential differences within generations as well as between them. (Abrams, 1992, pp.261-2).

This analysis does help to explain some puzzling features of the way generations behave. For example, concern has been expressed at the possibility of the old mobilising against the interests of the young, and the young breaking their part of the generational contract. In reality, neither of these things seem to be happening. The American Association of Retired Persons (AARP) is indeed a powerful organisation (second only to the United States branch of the Roman Catholic Church). However, despite its size and wealth, AARP can rarely mobilise its membership around any specific policy issue (Achenbaum, 1989). Or, to take another example, if one takes detailed studies of voter behaviour in so-called 'sunbelt states' such as Florida, where elderly voters constitute around one-quarter of the electorate, there is no evidence from available studies that older people represent a voting bloc or that they vote in a self - interested manner.

The British case is even more clear-cut. Despite the poverty of British pensioners and the government-led campaign against state pensions during the 1980s and early 1990s, the voting record of older people in the April 1992 election hardly suggested a pattern of militancy. Indeed, quite the reverse. Labour raised hopes of a 'demographic boost' to their chances with the promise of an immediate pensions increase on election and that future rises would once again be pegged to average wage as well as price rises (whichever rose faster). In fact, the Conservative vote amongst pensioners hardened - Conservative support amongst women 65 and over (theoretically one of the poorest groups) actually increased by 6 per cent in the period between the 1987 and 1992 election (*Sunday Times* 12 April 1992). This might be explained in generational equity terms on the basis that the Tories would give succour to the deserving old as opposed to the undeserving young. But the argument is tenuous and there is almost certainly a range of factors lying behind this result. It might also be noted in passing that amongst men aged 25-34 the Conservative vote remained remarkably steady - 41 per cent voting Tory in 1987; 40 per cent in 1992. This suggests, as indicated earlier, that age may be less important than a range of social factors (such as home ownership, social class, membership of a trade union) in interpreting voter behaviour (Walker, 1986; 1992). All these examples underline the case for a sociology of generations to be developed, complementary to the work of economists. Such work may well, following Abrams above, contribute to our understanding about the heterogeneity of the old and is likely, in addition, to have important implications for the development of economic and social policy.

Conclusion

The future of studies of ageing and older people will almost certainly be focused around the interplay between structural forces and changes to the self-identity of the old. How older people define themselves is open to negotiation in a way that was not the case even 10 years ago. This is for three main reasons: first, through awareness of the scale of demographic change; second, because of the evolution of retirement and the growth in the 1980s of early retirement from work; third, an emerging consciousness of age - reflected in the growth of social movements amongst some groups of older people. The interplay of these developments will undoubtedly transform our understanding of what it means to grow old, and will transform, as a consequence, how we study older people. The opportunities here will be considerable: for sociologists, the study of ageing will become mainstream rather than marginal - certainly, no study with the pretensions of understanding modernity can do so without an assessment of the social construction of old age and the challenge to self-identity in this period of the life course (Hockey and James, 1993). In social policy and social work, it is clear that a new approach to ageing will be necessary, focusing on the greater diversity of resources and lifestyles characteristic of this period (new studies of women by Bernard and Meade (1993) and Arber and Ginn (1992) are pioneering work in this area). Finally, in the field of community care, new approaches will also be necessary: if only because a significant piece of legislation - the 1990 National Health Service and Community Care Act - appears to be founded on a largely mythical view of family life and individual preferences amongst the old and their informal carers (Phillipson, 1992). The opportunities for research are certainly exciting and the aim of this chapter has been to provide an indication of some key areas of work for the years ahead.

References

Age Concern England (1992) *The Coming of Age in Europe*. London: Age Concern.

Abrams, P. (1982) *Historical Sociology*. Shepton Mallet: Open Books.

Arber, S. and Ginn, J. (1991) *Gender and Later Life*. London: Sage.

Bernard, M. and Meade, K. (1993) *Women Coming of Age*. London: Edward Arnold.

Bornat, J., Phillipson, C. and Ward, S. (1985) *A Manifesto for Old Age*. London: Pluto Press.

Bowling, A. and Cartwright, A. (1982) *Life After a Death*. London: Tavistock Books.

Bury, M. and Holmes, A. (1991) *Life After Ninety*. London: Routledge.

Estes, C. (1979) *The Aging Enterprise*. San Francisco: Josey-Bass.

Estes, C., Gerard, L., Zones, J. and Swan, J. (1984) *Political Economy, Health and Aging*. Boston, Little Brown.

Evandrou, M., Arber, S., Dale, A. and Gilbert, G.N. (1986) in C. Phillipson, M. Bernard and P. Strang (eds.) *Dependency and Interdependency in Old Age: Theoretical Perspectives and Policy Alternatives*. London, Croom Helm, pp.150-166.

Fennell, G., Phillipson, C. and Evers, H. (1988) *The Sociology of Old Age*. Milton Keynes: Open University Press.

Finch, J. (1989 *Family Obligations and Social Change*. Polity Press in association with Basil Blackwell.

Hockey, J. and James, A. (1993) *Growing Up and Growing Old*. London: Sage.

Jerrome, D. (1993) *Good Company*. Edinburgh: Edinburgh University Press.

Johnson, P., Conrad, C. and Thompson, D. (eds.) (1989) *Workers versus Pensioners*. Manchester: Manchester University Press in association with the Centre for Economic Policy Research.

Laczko, F. and Phillipson, C. (1991) *Changing Work and Retirement: Social Policy and the Older Worker*. Milton Keynes: Open University Press.

Longman, P. (1987) *Born to Pay: The New Politics of Ageing in America*. Boston: Houghton Mifflin.

Lee, G. (1985) 'Kinship and social support: the case of the United States', *Ageing and Society*, 5, pp.19-38.

Mannheim, K. (1952) 'The problem of generations' in *Essays on the Sociology of Knowledge*. London: Routledge and Kegan Paul.

Minkler, M. and Estes, C. (1991) *Critical Perspectives on Ageing*. San Francisco: Baywood Press.

Myles, J. (1984) *The Political Economy of Public Pensions*. Boston: Little, Brown.

Qureshi, H. and Walker, A. (1989) *The Caring Relationship*. London: Macmillan.

Phillipson, C. (1982) *Capitalism and the Construction of Old Age*. London: Macmillan Books.

Phillipson, C. (1990) 'Inter-generational relations: conflict or consensus in the twenty-first century', *Policy and Politics*, 19, pp.27-36.

Phillipson, C. (1991) 'The social construction of old age: perspectives from political economy', *Reviews in Clinical Gerontology*, 1, pp.403-410.

Phillipson, C. (1992) 'Challenging the 'spectre of old age': community care for older people in the 1990s' in N. Manning, and R. Page *Social Policy Review, 4*. Social Policy Association.

Phillipson, C. (1993) 'The sociology of retirement' in J. Bond, P. Coleman and S. Peace (eds.) *Ageing in Society*. Second Edition . London: Sage.

Phillipson, C. and Walker, A. (1986,) *Ageing and Social Policy*. Aldershot: Gower.

Schuller, T. and Bostyn, A.M. (1992) *Learning: Education, Training and Information in the Third Age*. The Carnegie Inquiry Into The Third Age. Research Paper No. 3. Dunfermline: The Carnegie United Kingdom Trust.

Szinovacz, M., Ekerdt, D. and Vinick, B. (1992) *Families and Retirement*. London: Sage

Salvage, A.V., Vetter, N.J. and Jones, D.A. (1989) 'Attitudes to hospital care among a community sample aged 75 and over', *Ageing and Ageing*, 17, pp.270-4.

Theroux, P. (1989) *Riding the Red Rooster*. London: Penguin Books.

Thompson, D. (1989) 'The welfare state and generation conflict: winners and losers' in P. Johnson, C. Conrad and D. Thompson (eds) (1989) *Workers Versus Pensioners*. Manchester: Manchester University Press in association with the Centre for Economic Policy Research.

Thompson, P., Itzin, C. and Abendstern, M. (1990) *I Don't Feel Old: The Experience of Later Life*. Oxford: Oxford University Press.

Townsend, P. (1957) *The Family Life of Old People*. London: Harmondsworth, Penguin.

Townsend, P. (1962) *The Last Refuge*. London: Routledge and Kegan Paul

Townsend, P. (1981) 'The structured dependency of the elderly: a creation of policy in the twentieth century', *Ageing and Society*, 1, pp.5-28.

Ungerson, C. (1987) *Policy is Personal: Sex, Gender and Informal Care*. London: Routledge, Kegan and Paul.

Walker, A. (1980) 'The social creation of poverty and dependency in old age', *Journal of Social Policy*, 9, pp.49-75.

Walker, A. (1981) 'Social policy, administration, and the construction of welfare', *Sociology*, 15.

Walker, A. (1986) 'The politics of ageing in Britain' in C. Phillipson, M. Bernard and P. Strang *Dependency and Interdependency in Old Age: Theoretical Perspectives and Policy Alternatives*. London: Croom Helm, pp.30-45.

Wall, R. (1992) 'Relationships between the generations in British families past and present' in C. Marsh and S. Arber (eds.) *Families and Households: Divisions and Change*. London: Macmillan, pp.63-85.

Wenger, C. (1984) *The Supportive Network: Coping with Old Age*. London: Allen and Unwin.

West, P., Illsley, R. and Kelman, H. (1984) 'Public preferences for the care of dependency groups', *Social Science and Medicine*, 18, pp.417-46.

Broken dreams:
the sociology of inter-generational
relations in Europe

BILL WILLIAMSON

The first forty years of life give us the text: the next thirty supply the commentary (Schopenhauer).

Introduction

In any given modern society, the relationships between people of different generations - particularly between the younger and older ones - can be characterised as being somewhere between two extremes. At one there is continuity, sympathy, mutual understanding and respect. At the other, there is discontinuity, dissonance and mutual incomprehension. The European Year of Solidarity Between the Generations offers a timely opportunity to consider these relationships in the specific circumstances of a continent undergoing profound social and political change. It is an opportunity to build a European dimension into discussions which have too often been only local and framed by the distinctive concerns of a particular society.

The European Community - which, to date at least, still excludes much of former Eastern Europe though it is unable to ignore its economic presence - is now an integrated economic community. As a unified market for goods and labour it facilitates movement and communication between different groups of people which, as little as forty years ago, would have been barely imaginable. Social identities, interests and life styles - including the attitudes of mind of different generations - are no longer unique to those of the society in which they live.

The European dimension to economic and social policies

now ensures that all aspects of the structure and functioning of modern societies have to be studied from a much broader perspective. The futures of European nation states are linked. The prevailing sense of what that future is or might be, will shape not only economic and social policies; it will shape, too, how people see themselves and how they construe what their personal and political interests are. It will shape their sense of the past, their hopes for the future, and their fears about the present. Necessarily, therefore, the boundaries people draw around their lives - those, for example, of nation, gender, class - and, for the purposes of this essay, generation - have to be explored in the wider context of the social changes sweeping European societies. It is against this backcloth that each generation comes to an understanding of the others and of their responsibilities towards them.

The central claim developed here is this: there is a subtle bond between the generations. However, it is improperly understood. It is obscured by ageist thinking. More fundamentally, it is damaged by those growing inequalities of wealth and opportunity which divide the societies of modern Europe and which erode the sympathy between people that is at the core of any credible ethic of mutual responsibility. The result, refracted through the political systems of modern states which typically favour the already well off, is that modern European governments have largely failed in so arranging their economic affairs and social policies that both the old and the young feel properly cared for and valued. Both groups too often rightly feel that they are being driven to the margins of their society. The old and the young perceive one another through a glass darkly, in ignorance of how their fates are linked and of the ways in which their interests can be jointly and effectively pursued.

The way to build the bridges of recognition and mutual comprehension is to help both the old and the young better understand the circumstances of their world. It is only on this basis that we can have confidence that future generations of young people will continue to feel they have a responsibility to care for and learn from those who are older. And it is only when those who are older acknowledge this that they, in their turn, will seek to arrange a better future for the young.

From the Angle of History

History tells us that in all ages the relationships between younger people and older people have been fraught. Aristotle complained that young people lacked moral restraint. In *The Winter's Tale*, Shakespeare observed that youth - the period between the ages ten and twenty-three - was one preoccupied with 'getting wenches with child, wronging the ancientry, stealing, fighting'.

It is a safe conclusion that the behaviour of young people comes to be seen as a particular problem when there is some underlying crisis in the society in which they live. When the future prospects of a society are in doubt, the question becomes pressing: how well equipped are the young to defend the values of that society in the uncertain times ahead? A good illustration of this, analysed by Hendrick (1990), is given in the modern period in the development of the 'boy labour' problem. This dates from the last decade of the last and first two decades of this century. Working class youth became a problem to employers and middle class philanthropists because the chaotic conditions of their labour undermined their morality and ultimately - at least, so it was believed - rendered them dangerous to the prevailing social order. These concerns persisted into the 1920s and 1930s.

In the period since the Second World War, there have been several spasms of anxiety over the behaviour of the young: in the 1950s the concern over teddy boys, in the 1960s over student radicals and mods and rockers, and in the 1970s over a whole series of youth styles, particularly those of punks and skinheads. The common thread to these reactions was a fear that the young no longer respected the prevailing moral standards of society and were thus unable to carry them on.

In the 1980s, much was written about alienated and marginalised young people, who turn to drugs and violence for their fun and seemed to reject society's mainstream values. Never far from these concerns was a fundamental worry about the performance of the economy which translated into forms of moral panic and attempts to tighten the controls on the young and bring order to their world.

In the cold climate of the 1990s, young people - especially the unemployed among them - have come into view again as the ill-educated architects of their own fate. That is in Britain, where politicians of the ruling party are all too willing to blame the poor for their poverty. Elsewhere in Europe, particularly in the former communist states of Eastern Europe, some young people - the skin heads and neo-Nazis - are seen to be the sole cause of increasing levels of politically motivated attacks on foreigners, asylum seekers and migrants. These phenomena, however, actually require a much broader analysis of civil rights issues and institutional racism. Throughout Europe, it nevertheless remains true that levels of unemployment among young people are nearly always double the adult rate and for many young people the future is indeed a bleak one.

There is no necessity in this. There is no economic law which compels such outcomes. Social policies could be devised which would alter materially the life chances of the young. Whether such policies will ever be put in place depends, however, on the ways in which those with power in the older generations perceive the needs and interests of the young. This is, in part, a matter of the ways in which older generations have themselves experienced the world and of their beliefs about how it can be changed. It is also a question of how the young identify their own needs, articulate their interests, and seek to realise them (or not, as the case may be) through the political institutions of their society. For both young and old, it is a question of how they make sense of their experience.

From the Angle of Experience

Older people and young people necessarily perceive the world in different ways. There is an inevitable tension between them, centred on striking the right balance between control and autonomy. The parental generation of a society is compelled to exert control over the young. The drive to maturity requires the young to assert their independence and autonomy: first from their parents, then their teachers and, later, from those in authority over them at work and in the community. What form this tension takes is something which changes through time, varies between societies, and is subject to a whole range of historical contingencies reflecting the demographic, economic, political and cultural circumstances of a society.

Nevertheless, young people and older people experience the world in different ways. Because of differences in life span, people from different generations have different memories and

have assembled the fundamental meaning of their lives in different ways. Secondly, they face different circumstances and have, literally, different life chances. Thirdly, they have different views of and attitudes towards the future. The complexity of this becomes almost baffling when it is acknowledged that within each generation there are further differences between people dependent on their gender, class background, ethnic origin, education and employment.

Such divisions shape the ways in which people think about one another and attach significance to differences of age. In British society, there is great ambiguity in age status. Ronald Blythe in his moving study of old age, *The View in Winter*, alluded to this when he wrote: 'Unable to love the old, we approach them via sentiment, duty and an eye to our own eventual decline'. (1981, p.24)

To be old, except under special circumstances, is not usually something which elicits respect in younger people. Philip Larkin's poem, 'The Old Fools' illustrates this rather well. His portrait of the elderly in an old people's home - of people with 'prune face' pissing themselves, living in a dream with an air of 'baffled absence' - is a savage depiction by a middle-aged man of the mental state of the frail elderly people. There can be no point, the poem proclaims, in living a life in such a 'hideous inverted childhood'.

It seems at first a deeply unsympathetic poem but is redeemed in its last line when Larkin projects himself and, by implication, the rest of us as well, into that same future state he has just described. We shall all find out what it is like !

The world of the old people's home which Larkin described is part of a society which deals with a significant number of its elderly people by segregating them. In western Europe, societies are essentially urban, with ageing populations and high levels of social and geographic mobility which break up extended families and unsettle patterns of communal life. Consequently, more and more people will experience old age apart from their families. For many, it will be a bitter disappointment at odds with their memories of hard fought hopes to build a better world.

For too many people, the experience of being elderly will also be one of being poor. The scandal of poverty in old age is a long standing one. In Britain it was tellingly exposed by Peter

Townsend in the 1950s and 1960s. Much has changed since then; the nineteenth century poor law institutions in which many were housed have been pulled down but the problems of poverty and inequality in old age have not been solved. And there is an ironic gender twist to it all: women live longer than men so that the disadvantages of their gender status persist for many into ripe old age.

The tragedy in this is not just that many old people cannot live decently in an increasingly wealthy society; it is also that the wealth of their experience and knowledge cannot be properly capitalised. Those who are now retired in modern Europe represent generations of people who have experienced some of the most profound transformations of the twentieth century. Ronald Blythe noted that the First World War was now passing out of living memory. So, too, we might add, are the Means Test, inter-war Fascism, the League of Nations and heroic struggles against totalitarianism both in the East and the West.

Many old people in modern Europe look back with considerable dismay at the changes which have occurred in their society. Regret at how things have turned out, as Jeremy Seabrook and others, have recorded in *What Went Wrong?* (1978) is a commonly articulated sentiment. This is not regret about having escaped grinding poverty or domestic violence or drudgery or poor, insanitary housing. It is much more that people no longer value one another; it is a regret about the quality of personal relationships and hopes.

We are too close to the revolutions of 1989 in Eastern Europe to know how older people there view the past. There must be hundreds of thousands of ex-communists who now feel their lives and their achievements - in defeating Fascism and building Socialism - have been betrayed. There are strong hints that this is the case. And among millions who did not support the communist states, but who were compelled to live their lives under them, there must be many who harbour a strong feeling of resentment about the opportunities they have missed and the indignities they believe they have suffered. These issues are being actively explored now in Germany (see, for example, Maaz, 1991), as people in a reunified nation come to terms once more with their past.

Who can tell how they will come to view the younger generations around them - with bemusement? hostility?

mistrust? Philip Larkin provides another clue about how the young were perceived in the late 1960s. In his poem, 'Going Going', he conjured up an England polluted by greed and materialism. It would become the first slum of Europe because the 'crowd is young in the M1 cafe' and 'their kids are screaming for more'. And in the poem, 'Annus Mirabilis' (1974), he cast a wry look at post-Chatterley sexual morality among the young. Sexual intercourse, he said, began in 1963 - between the Chatterley ban and the Beatles' first LP. The point, though, was that it was too late for him !

Larkin's sentiments are part of a structure of feeling in Britain which was perhaps unique to one section of the educated middle class who resented post-war affluence for the majority of the population. Larkin's friend, Kingsley Amis, shared this view and complained in the early sixties about the decline in cultural standards. The prospect of an expanded university system appalled him. More students would mean worse students in his view.

The perceptions of older people from a working class background of the behaviour and needs of young people has been well documented by sociologists as being centred on the theme of control and discipline. In her study, *A Sociology of Contemporary Cultural Change,* Bernice Martin (1981) characterised working class culture as a 'culture of control'. This was a culture with firm boundaries, strict standards, and a strong distaste for disorder; in its reaction to the youth cultures of the post-war world, the stress was placed on the need to restore order and a narrow version of normality.

One potent model for this, until 1958, had of course been national service, during which young men were subject to the discipline of the sergeant major: a mixture of mindless harassment, brute authoritarianism, and spit and polish. It was a model framed, too, by memories of their old childhood discipline in much harsher times when corporal punishment in school and firm discipline at home were the norm. The steady rise of juvenile crime, during the 1960s and subsequently, nurtured such controlling sentiments.

National service ended in Britain in the late 1950s; it continues to be part of the experience of many young people in mainland Europe. And for young people in the former communist states of Eastern Europe, national service was combined with Cold War propaganda to instil strong nationalist sentiments and socialist pride among the heroes' children. It is a sad fact that many young people in Eastern Europe, having been denied a critical political education and having been led to think of their own societies as standing at a pinnacle of human development, became disenchanted with politics. They either then ignored it, or else were so blinded to the flaws of their own society that they now seek explanations for their plight in the scapegoating of foreigners and gypsies.

The young of the East, who now look so optimistically towards a model of their future based on the experience of the West, have been nurtured in a much tighter culture of control which has undermined their autonomy and self-confidence. The danger is that they will seek to compensate for this through a desperate search for material possessions and will feel frustrated by their inability to acquire them. How they will then see their elders, many of whom they will regard as collaborators, is anyone's guess.

This is not the place to debate these issues; they need only be noted as manifestations of the changing context in which one generation frames a view of those to follow them. Britain in the 1960s was a society in which strong generational differences were emerging and being consolidated. Given the class structure of the country, they were typically compounded by mistrust, prejudice and misrecognition.

Continental European countries - especially those of the developed North and in particular France, Germany and the Netherlands - experienced the changes of post-war Europe in different ways. Less hamstrung by the social institutions of a class society, they knuckled down to reconstruction and to building new kinds of societies, with much less sentimentality about the past. The outcome, during the late 1950s and 1960s, was the growth of affluent societies and of a generation of well-educated, confident young people willing to challenge politically the universities in which they were being taught and, in France, to bring down a government.

What perceptions older age groups are now forming about the young is a matter for conjecture. My suspicion is that these cover a mixture of anxiety, fear and despair on the one hand and, on the other (but from different sections of the adult population) - sympathy and concern that the young are particularly disadvantaged and deserve much better opportunities for education, training and employment. Nor is this a uniquely British pattern. As youth unemployment rises throughout the continent, East-West gradients of disadvantage are becoming much more obvious. The consequences for the ways in which some young people then make sense of their world are frightening to imagine. It is becoming clearer that the relationships between generations and their perceptions of one another are altering fundamentally.

Seen from the angle of young people, history has a different significance. For the younger generations of Europe, especially in the West, their experience of change has been one of improvement and an extension of their realm of freedom. Youth cultures are strong symbolic boundaries which separate the experience of different generations. The future is much more important to the young and most of them tacitly assume, unless there is evidence to the contrary (as there is for a growing number of young people), that the contract they have with the older generation will be honoured. That contract is to study and to work so that those who are older will protect them, promote them, and guarantee their rights and freedoms. The longer term goal is to take their own responsible place in society after their period of freedom.

The history of the futures available to successive post-war generations has been, for the most part, an optimistic one. In the East, the heroes' children were building socialism. They were the heirs to a great tradition of struggle to transform capitalism and build a new culture. In the West, they were the beneficiaries of affluence, opportunity and the Welfare State. Until the mid 1970s, throughout Europe, young people experienced full employment and steadily increasing numbers of them gained entry into higher education.

There were great variations in the patterns of their opportunity between East and West and among the states of each of the Great Power blocs. In the East, for example, the opportunities for the children of working people to gain entry to further and higher education increased much faster than they did in the West, but with more emphasis on job-related education and training. On the Continent, a greater proportion of the relevant age groups entered higher education than in Britain, where elitist traditions of higher education continued despite the expansion of the system in the 1960s. However, with the exception of young people from families from the unskilled working class, opportunities for education to promote their social mobility steadily increased.

The result, as studies of social mobility have shown, is not that class inequalities altered fundamentally, but that social movement did take place which distinguished clearly the experience of one generation from another. For many working class grammar schoolstudents in Britain, the experience was profound. It alienated them from their parents and their class, both of origin and destination, inducing a sense of marginality. The poet, Tony Harrison, comments on this most poignantly in a moving sequence of sonnets, just as Richard Hoggart had done a generation earlier. He notes all the languages he can now speak. They include Latin and Greek, but not the one he can't bone up on now 'and that's mi mam's' (1985, p.118).

Nevertheless, for those who grew to early adulthood before the late 1970s and early 1980s, in contrast to the experience of many young people now, there was hope. This hope extended to jobs, education, a decent standard of living and of being able to join in a society whose horizons seemed to be expanding. For those who left school early, there was still the hope of work and a place in the community as citizens. It may have been a cramped and ordered world, especially for young women, but they had a place in it.

For those coming to maturity now in the 1990s, the prospects are very different. Unemployment is the scourge of this generation and it is not a problem likely to be solved by economic growth alone. The advanced economies, locked in global competition among themselves, are driven by a technological imperative to reduce employment. Most western governments, too, are driven by a political imperative to reduce public spending. The reasons for doing so are very different in different states - in Germany to cope with the escalating costs of the *Wiedervereinigung*, or unification; in Britain to implement a dominant ideological prejudice and reduce a deficit in public finances; in Italy to reduce the size of the state itself. In all cases there is the necessity to improve productivity and competitiveness and to face the challenge from the Pacific Rim economies.

These are societies structured to generate inequalities as

an inevitable consequence of how their economies work and of the way power is distributed within them. It is not surprising, therefore, that the costs of the restructuring of social expenditures are everywhere falling on those who can most easily be marginalised. They constitute a complex grouping of people but include the poor, the old, those without the skills a modern economy requires and many groups of young people without the education or training they need to find jobs.

There are spatial patterns to social deprivation. The more traditional industrial regions of Europe concentrate within themselves some of the highest levels of social deprivation. Within the towns and cities of those regions, there are social areas of intense poverty and hopelessness, of ageing populations, and ghettoes of long term youth unemployment. These are breeding-ground conditions for crime and delinquency, drug misuse and, under some conditions, racial violence.

This is all well enough known. Not so clear is how different groups of people make sense of it. There are emerging in Europe new forms of ethnic nationalism which are recasting political identities in very dangerous ways. There is a generational aspect to this: those with memories of pre-war Fascism and of Nazism can sense the dangers. Those for whom the Holocaust is history cannot read the signs in quite the same way. The neo-Nazi skinheads of some of the towns and cities of former East Germany have no investment in the future of a society which denies them jobs and opportunity. Their growing commitment is to a society of the past, a Germany cleansed of foreigners.

But who else will it exclude ? Who else does not fit into the world they imagine in the future ? Europe is infected at the moment by what Stuart Hall has called, 'ethnic and cultural absolutism' (1992). That is one problem. The social differentiation which exists between the generations is another, but they are linked. As life expectancies increase, as the demographic decline in the numbers of young people continues, the social and cultural gap between the generations could widen considerably - eroding the subtle bonds of sympathy, mutual recognition and support which should exist between them. Neither will be able to learn from the other or share in the struggles - for the justice, social security, decent housing, and the ability to participate in society - that are the hallmarks of a decent society.

Conclusion

There is no inevitability to such developments; the future could be different. But it first has to be imagined. This presupposes a degree of sympathy for the needs of others and an ability on the part of people from different generations to look to each others' needs. Whether they can do so depends on the kind and quality of contact they have. In societies which isolate the old and insulate the young, such sympathy across the generations cannot be nurtured. Re-connected with one another through genuine opportunities to care, to learn from each other's experience, to debate the past and the future, to fight for just causes together, would promise a very different future. The challenge is to build into that future, not only a concern for family and friends, but for what Michael Ignatieff has described as 'the needs of strangers' (1984). And in the world we live in, this must include not only strangers in other towns, but in other countries. The European Year of Solidarity Between Generations is a good start to promote the kind of dialogue that is needed. The young and the old may live in different countries, but they share the same world. Inevitably their fates are linked.

References

Blythe, R. (1981) *The View in Winter.* Harmondsworth: Penguin Books.

Hall, S. (1992) 'Our mongrel selves', *New Statesman and Society*, 19 June, p.6

Harrison, T. (1985) *Selected poems.* Harmondsworth: Penguin Books.

Hendrick, H. (1990) *Images of Youth: Age, Class, and the Male Youth Problem 1880-1920.* Oxford: Clarendon Press.

Ignatieff, M. (1984) *The Needs of Strangers.* London: Chatto and Windus.

Larkin, P. (1974) *High Windows.* London: Faber and Faber.

Maaz, H.J. (1990) *Der Gefühlsstau: Ein Psychogramm der D.D.R.* Berlin: Argon Verlag.

Martin, B. (1981) *A Sociology of Contemporary Cultural Change.* Oxford: Blackwell.

Seabrook, J. (1978) *What Went Wrong?* London: Gollanz.

The demography of ageing in Europe

JOHN I. CLARKE

Definitions

Ageing of a population merely means the increase in the proportion of the elderly in relation to younger age-groups. Thus the main indicator is the percentage of the population over a certain age. But what age? There are no hard and fast definitions of old age, the elderly, the very old or the very elderly, and they tend to change with time. The 1982 World Assembly on Ageing defined the aged population as those aged 60 and over, a rather low threshold by European standards, possibly influenced by the fact that most of the poorer countries in the world have relatively few old people and that if a higher age was selected their percentages of old people would be very low.

In Britain, it is more common to consider 65 as the threshold of old age, probably because it was the traditional age of retirement and pensions for men; but for similar reasons 60 has been used as the threshold for women, a curious differential when women are living longer than men. In fact, many men are retiring prematurely or are being made redundant and many women continue working after 60. Moreover, as both sexes are enjoying longer lives, the perceptions and proposed definitions of old age are changing, especially because of the growing proportions of populations aged 75 and over and 85 and over. Indeed, the old age-group can no longer be regarded as a single homogeneous entity, for there is a great difference between the younger aged and the older aged in terms of their activities, health, medical and housing needs, independence and social integration/segregation.

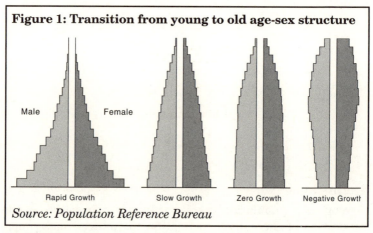

Figure 1: Transition from young to old age-sex structure

Male   Female

Rapid Growth   Slow Growth   Zero Growth   Negative Growth

Source: Population Reference Bureau

Analysis

Demographic ageing is usually analysed, especially internationally, by reference to three age-groups, say 0-14, 15-64 and 65 and over, broadly reflecting the traditional ages of infancy/schooling, economic activity and retirement. The thresholds are sometimes altered to reflect rising ages of school leaving and earlier ages of retirement; so 0-19 is sometimes used for infants and adolescents, and 15-59, 19-59 and 19-64 for adults (occasionally divided into younger adults, e.g. 15-34, and older adults, e.g. 35-64)

The three arbitrary age-groups are also often used to calculate the dependency ratio, by dividing the number aged 0-14 plus those aged 65 and over by the number aged 15-64. Designed crudely as the ratio of the economically dependent part of the population to the productive part, the dependency ratio may also be decomposed to analyse child dependency and old age dependency (sometimes known as the old-age index), because the cost 'burdens' of the two are different. Generally, high old age dependency implies higher costs to the state, whereas high child dependency implies higher costs to the family or household.

The three age-groups and dependency ratios are only simple crude indices of the complexities of age-sex structure which reveals the composition of a population according to the number or proportion of males or females at each age or quinquennial age-group. The age-sex structure may be sensitively analysed by reference to the so-called population pyramid. The term 'pyramid' is really only appropriate for rapidly growing youthful populations, as the slowing down of population growth and the accompanying ageing of population tends to transform the pyramid into a bell-shaped or pear-shaped or even rectangular figure as the younger age-groups diminish and the older age-groups increase (Fig. 1). The population pyramid thus changes from being 'progressive' to 'regressive'. Although the population pyramid has many advantages in depicting the diversity of age and sex structure, unfortunately it is not very satisfactory for the oldest age-group, say 85 and over, which is usually open-ended and not really comparable with the younger age-groups.

Process of Ageing

Ageing of a population reflects the interplay of the three dynamic elements of fertility (the occurrence of live births), mortality (the occurrence of deaths) and the balance of in- and out-migration. Ageing means a more rapid growth or slower decline of the older age-groups in relation to the remainder of the population. It may therefore result from the following:

1. *Ageing at the base* (of the population pyramid): a slowing down in population growth at younger ages caused by long-term fertility decline, generally the key factor in ageing of national populations;
2. *Ageing at the top* (of the population pyramid): an increase in growth at older ages by mortality decline among them, a factor gaining importance in the more developed countries; and
3. *Age-sex selective migration*, notably the movement in or out of older migrants for retirement, or more often the movement of younger migrants for work or a change of housing, a factor which is particularly important at the local rather than the national level, except for micro-states such as Luxembourg, Monaco and Andorra.

Migration is an irregular phenomenon and has less even effects upon the population pyramid than long-term trends in fertility and mortality, but the ageing of populations is also affected by past fluctuations in fertility and mortality, varying the numbers in the age cohorts and causing indentations and

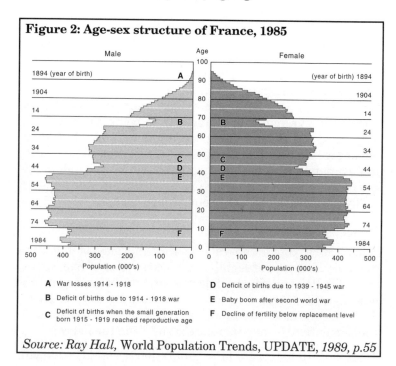

Figure 2: Age-sex structure of France, 1985

A War losses 1914 - 1918
B Deficit of births due to 1914 - 1918 war
C Deficit of births when the small generation born 1915 - 1919 reached reproductive age
D Deficit of births due to 1939 - 1945 war
E Baby boom after second world war
F Decline of fertility below replacement level

Source: Ray Hall, World Population Trends, UPDATE, *1989, p.55*

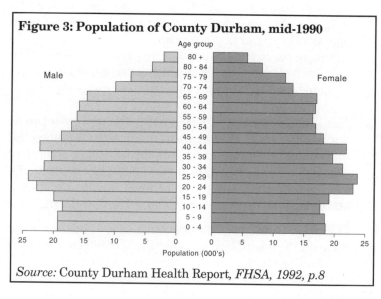

Figure 3: Population of County Durham, mid-1990

Source: County Durham Health Report, *FHSA, 1992, p.8*

protrusions in population pyramids. Countries like France (Fig. 2) and Germany therefore have extremely serrated age-sex pyramids reflecting war losses and birth deficits during the two world wars, post-war baby booms and depressions. The population pyramid of County Durham (Fig. 3) is similarly serrated. Consequently, the annual numbers entering the old and very old age-groups are very irregular, indicative of the marked demographic changes that took place during the century. The population of a country may experience a considerable increase in the numbers aged 75 and over, but not in those aged 65 and over - much depends upon its demographic characteristics.

Demographic Transition and Ageing

Ageing is not a new phenomenon in Europe, or indeed in more developed countries (MDCs) as a whole. It was an inevitable consequence of the demographic transition from high to low birth and death rates which Europe experienced over a lengthy period from the late eighteenth century to the first half of the twentieth century. The process was generally initiated by a decline in death rates especially of young people, which meant that populations became more youthful with broader bases to the population pyramids. It was only when the birth rates subsequently declined that the ageing process really got under way.

Of course, demographic transition took place at different times and rates within Europe, earlier and slower in northern and western Europe, and later and more rapidly in southern and eastern Europe. Although the process had begun earliest in France, by the beginning of the Second World War most of northern and western Europe (and indeed North America) had achieved low levels of fertility. The rest of the continent followed suit at different rates during the post-war period, so that now fertility and mortality are low almost everywhere except in Albania, which is decades behind, not only demographically.

The effect upon ageing is striking. With 13 per cent or about 70 million aged 65 and over, Europe (excluding the former USSR) is the continent with the highest proportion of elderly people. Slightly above the average for the MDCs as a whole (12 per cent), it is more than twice the world average (6 per cent), and three times the average for the less developed

Table 1
Ageing in selected Council of Europe countries, 1950-2025

| | % aged 65 and over | | | |
	1950	1970	1990	2025
Austria	11	14	15	22
Belgium	11	13	15	23
Denmark	9	12	16	23
France	12	13	14	21
F.Rep. Germany	9	13	15	24
Greece	7	11	14	21
Iceland	8	9	11	18
Ireland	11	11	11	13
Italy	8	11	14	23
Liechtenstein	8	8	10	
Luxembourg	10	13	13	23
Malta	6	9	10	18
Netherlands	8	10	13	21
Norway	10	13	16	21
Portugal	7	10	13	18
Spain	7	10	13	19
Sweden	10	14	18	22
Switzerland	10	11	15	23
UK	11	13	16	19

countries (LDCs) in most of which demographic transition has only occurred since mid-century. In some LDCs old people account for only 1 per cent (e.g. Qatar, United Arab Emirates) or 2 per cent (e.g. Nigeria, Kenya, Zambia) of the population. In contrast, in Britain, the percentage aged 65 and over is now as high as 16, comparable with Norway and Denmark, and approaching the percentage (19) aged 0-14; but Sweden has the oldest population of any country in the world, with both the young and the old accounting for 18 per cent of the total population.

This was not always the case, for until the 1960s France had the oldest population of all the major countries in the world. At the beginning of the century it had about 8 per cent elderly (cf. UK less than 5 per cent), and in 1950 11.8 per cent

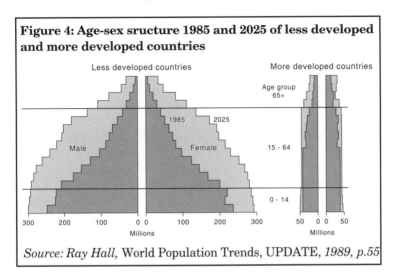

Figure 4: Age-sex sructure 1985 and 2025 of less developed and more developed countries

Source: Ray Hall, World Population Trends, UPDATE, *1989, p.55*

(cf. UK 10.7 per cent). Since the 1960s France has enjoyed prolonged peace, slower than average fertility decline and much immigration from overseas, and consequently it has been rapidly overhauled in ageing by many other European countries which experienced faster fertility decline (Table 1). Long-term projections to the year 2025 suggest that the aged population of the Economic Commission for Europe (ECE) region will steadily increase by about 75 per cent from 1990. Moreover, more than a dozen European countries, not including the United Kingdom, are expected to have over 20 per cent of their populations aged 65 and over, and all the main countries in northern, western and southern Europe are likely to have percentages of elderly population equal to or more than Sweden today. Projections for the years 2005 and 2025, which involve making assumptions about births as well as deaths, suggest that the MDCs will experience a gradual shift to a more rectangular population pyramid, initially to more older adults and then to more old people (Fig. 4). The long-term projection is far from being a certainty but is nevertheless very striking, though not for every country. The notable exception is Ireland, whose demographic characteristics have differed considerably from most other European countries, especially because of relatively high fertility and substantial emigration. Similarly, the situation is very different in eastern Europe, where the proportions of old people are generally lower, especially in Albania, the former Yugoslavia, Poland and Romania.

The Very Old

In most European countries the very old or oldest old age-groups (usually taken as 75 and over, but some times as 80 and over) have grown more rapidly than the younger old age-groups, reflecting improved survival at advanced ages and also the larger size of the cohorts born in the early decades of this century. During the period 1901-91 the proportion aged 75 and over increased by more than five-fold in England and Wales, and those aged 85 and over by eight-fold, but the absolute numbers have multiplied by much more. There were only 44 thousand aged 85 and over in 1901; now there are more than 900 thousand. These remarkable increases are likely to continue, and projections suggest that over the period 1989-2025 those aged 75-84 will increase by 35 per cent and those aged 85 and over will increase by 76 per cent. In County Durham alone those aged 85 and over will probably increase by 40 per cent during the 1990s.

Of course, in facing a future in which one-tenth of its population is aged 75 or more, Britain is not alone. Most of the countries of northern and western Europe are in a similar position, with problems of increasing demands upon their health and social support systems. The problems will be particularly concentrated in the four most populous countries - Germany (80m in 1991) UK (58m), Italy (58m) and France (57m) - which contain almost exactly half of the population of Europe excluding the former USSR, but a much higher proportion of the elderly and very old.

Older Women

Although high and rising life expectancies have not been the main cause of ageing in Europe in the past, they are playing an increasing role, as all countries are experiencing gains in their life expectancies at birth. Everywhere in Europe the average is over 70, and is as high as 78 in Sweden and Switzerland (cf. 75 in the UK).

The main feature is the marked and generally widening difference between the life expectancies of males and females, which is generally 4 to 8 years despite recent indications that sex differentials in mortality have narrowed slightly. Data from the late 1980s showed that in several European countries (Switzerland, France, Sweden, Iceland, Netherlands, Norway) female life expectancy was about 80, but only in Iceland had male life expectancy reached 75. In the UK the comparable figures were 78 and 72, in contrast with Japan 82 and 76.

Differential life expectancy means that the proportion of women increases with age. In the ECE region as a whole, there are about six older men aged 60 and over for every ten women of comparable age, but at 80 the ratio drops to four, and at 100 it is less than two. In short, women are preponderant amongst older populations, and this results in a growing proportion living alone.

Distribution

The above generalisations are mostly relevant to the countries of Europe as political units, but they show great individual diversity in their internal population distribution. Some populations like Belgium, Germany and the Netherlands are nine-tenths urban while Portugal is only one-third urban and the proportions of old people vary as between town and country. Rural populations usually have a higher proportion of old people than urban populations, particularly through age selective migration of younger people to towns, but this is not the case in Austria, Denmark, Netherlands and Switzerland. Much depends upon differential patterns of natural increase, migration, housing and social facilities.

In Britain, retirement migration to coastal resorts, inland spas and tourist areas has greatly influenced the distribution of the elderly, with strong pockets of concentration, in contrast to active manufacturing areas. Even locally there are substantial variations. For example, in County Durham although the 1991 census revealed that 6.3 per cent of the population of North Durham were aged 75 and over, in Elvet ward it was 13 per cent, and in Annfield Plain and Seaham 12 per cent.

Conclusion

Demographic transition, especially fertility decline, has ensured that Europe's population has aged markedly, but continued low levels of fertility along with declining mortality mean that over the next few decades the process will continue much further. In particular, further mortality declines will lead to a major increase in the numbers and proportions of very old. The age-sex selectivity of migration will have a further sorting effect, so that geographical patterns of ageing will remain uneven and complicated.

The European Population Conference held in Geneva in March 1993 showed that European countries are becoming much more conscious of the social, economic and political implications of ageing. They are realising that the aged are an important element in their human resources. The conference encouraged them to develop policies which reflect changes in the composition of their labour forces, to consider the valuable contribution that the elderly can make to society, to face up to the growing expenditure on their pensions and health services, to enable them to remain self-reliant and independent as long as possible, and to provide adequate resources for their care. Governments will need to make considerable adjustments in order to achieve these goals.

Why so many old?

PETER KAIM-CAUDLE

Changes in Size, Sex and Age Composition since 1901

In this century the population of England and Wales increased by just over one half while the number of younger elderly (65-74 years) increased four fold and that of the very elderly (75 years plus) increased eight fold (see Table I). This resulted in the proportion of the elderly in the population rising, from not quite five per cent to nearly 16 per cent (see Table 2). In this chapter these changes will be discussed and an attempt will be made to explain them.

During these nine decades the age and sex composition of the elderly changed quite markedly. The elderly have become more elderly, and more of them are now female. In 1901 the very elderly were 29 per cent of the elderly population; by 1991 this had increased to 44 per cent. The preponderance of females amongst the very elderly, but not amongst the younger elderly, increased substantially. In 1901 there were 144 females for every 100 males. By 1991 this ratio had increased to 190 so that at present there are almost twice as many females as males amongst the very elderly.

In 1901 there were 43 very old females for every 100 younger elderly females. By 1991 this proportion had increased to 95, so that in 1991 the number of women aged 75 years and older was approximately the same as that of women aged 65-75 years. For males the position was rather different. In 1901 there had been 38 very elderly males for every 100 younger elderly males - much the same ratio as for females - but by 1991 this proportion had increased to only 61, so that amongst males the younger elderly still greatly exceeded the very elderly.

These changes in the age and sex composition were due to changes in mortality rates, especially the greater decline in female than male rates. Immigration and emigration during

Table 1
Elderly population by sex, 1901 and 1991, England and Wales (millions)

	1901			1991			Ratio of 1991 on 1901		
	P	M	F	P	M	F	P	M	F
Younger elderly									
(65-74 yrs)	1.08	.48	.60	4.52	2.03	2.49	4.2	4.2	4.2
Very elderly									
(75 yrs plus)	.44	.18	.26	3.60	1.24	2.36	8.2	6.9	9.1
All elderly	1.52	.66	.86	8.12	3.27	4.85	5.3	5.0	5.6
Total pop'n	32.5	15.7	16.8	51.0	24.9	26.1	1.6	1.6	1.6

Notes: P - Persons, M - Male, F - Female
Sources: 1901, Statistical Abstract of the UK No. 76, *Table 13;*
1991, OPCS Population Trends No. 70, *1992 Table 6.*

Table 2
Elderly population by sex as proportion of total population, 1901 and 1991, England and Wales

	1901			1991			1991 increase over 1901		
	P %	M %	F %	P %	M %	F %	P %	M %	F %
Younger elderly									
(65-74 yrs)	3.3	3.0	3.6	8.8	8.2	9.5	5.5	5.2	5.9
Very elderly									
(75 yrs plus)	1.4	1.2	1.5	7.1	5.0	9.0	5.7	3.8	7.5
All elderly	4.7	4.2	5.1	15.9	13.2	18.5	11.2	9.0	13.4
Total Pop'n	100	100	100	100	100	100	100	100	100

Notes: As in Table 1.   Sources: Derived from Table 1

this period had not been on a sufficient scale to make any marked difference and the annual fluctuations in the proportion of male to female births diverge only minimally from the ratio of 51 to 49.

Importance of Differential Sex and Age Mortalities

The popular view that the increase in the number and proportion of elderly people in the population is due mainly to the elderly living longer is quite erroneous. The increase in the average expectation of life at the age of 65 years explains only a quite small proportion of the increase in the number of elderly people. In 1901 a man could expect to live on average another 10.8 years after his 65th birthday while a woman could expect to live another 12.0 years - a sex difference of 1.2 years in favour of women. These expected years of survival were much the same as men and women had experienced during the previous 70 years. Between 1901 and 1951 the average expectation of life of men increased to 11.7 years, that is by some eight per cent and that of females to 14.3 years, that is by 19 per cent.

In 1991 the average expectation of life at the age of 65 years was 14.0 years for men and 17.8 years for women - the sex difference had increased to 3.8 years. Thus during this century, the longevity of men after 65 years increased by only 30 per cent while that of women increased by 48 per cent. The decline in mortality amongst the elderly was less than amongst the younger age groups. This is well illustrated by an extreme example: In England and Wales in 1901 male mortality in the first year of life was 160 per 1,000 births; ninety years later it was eight per 1,000, a decrease of 95 per cent. During the same period the mortality rate for men aged 75 to 85 years decreased from 144 to 94 per 1,000 a decrease of 35 per cent. Amongst the elderly mortality declined at all ages and both sexes, but the decline was substantially greater amongst women than men and greater during the last four decades than the previous five decades.

Changes in general mortality cannot be attributed in quantitative terms to specific factors. The factors which contribute to a decline or increase in mortality are generally, though not invariably, known but the relative importance of such factors as improvements in diet, less crowded housing or higher standards of individual health services cannot be ascertained with any degree of accuracy. The reduction in mortality amongst the elderly in this century will have been partly due to the changes in environment and behaviour which reduced mortality at all ages but it seems probable that the improvements in quality and quantity of individual health services benefited the elderly more than the younger age groups. This informed guess is quite compatible with the fact that in the mid 1980s the elderly 14 per cent of the population occupied 60 per cent of the non-maternity and non-psychiatric NHS hospital beds (mainly in acute hospitals) and were the major recipients of prescription medicines.

The increase in the longevity of the elderly during this century would have increased their number by about 40 per cent if everything else had remained unaltered, while their actual number increased more than five fold.

The increase in the number of men and women who survive to attain old age is much more important in explaining the increase in the number of elderly than the increase in longevity of the elderly. In this century there has been a substantial decline in mortality at all ages and for both sexes but, as has already been mentioned, the decline was greater at the early years of life and markedly greater for females than for males. In 1901, out of 100 female born 87 survived to their first birthday. This is about the same proportion as in 1991 survived to their 65th birthday. An increase in the life of an older woman merely increases her life, while the survival of a younger woman or a baby girl enables her to bear children and to contribute to an increase in the population.

The increase in the proportion of men and women who survive to the age of 65 years has been quite remarkable - for men from 37 per cent in 1901-1905 (Case 1970) to 78 per cent in 1989 while the corresponding increase for women was from 44 per cent to 86 per cent. To explain these phenomena would require answers to two questions: Why has female mortality declined more rapidly than male mortality, and what are the major causes which resulted in the decline of mortality?

More Rapid Decline in Female Mortality

To the first question there is no satisfactory answer. Five characteristics of the phenomenon of higher male than female death rates are well established. They have been notable ever since records have been kept; male rates have exceeded female rates at all times and at all ages (with quite minor and temporary exceptions); in this century the differences between male and female rates have increased for every age group; at present, for the great majority of diseases in all age groups, male age specific death rates exceed female rates; and lastly these four characteristics are not peculiar to England and Wales, but are common to other European countries. The reasons for these sex differential death rates have not necessarily been the same at all times, nor will they have been the same for all diseases. The higher male death rates for lung cancer and cirrhosis of the liver are almost certainly due to men smoking and drinking alcohol more than women. The higher male death rate for the 15-24 years age group is largely due to men suffering more accidents.

While there is no satisfactory explanation of why the general death rates of females are and always have been lower than those of males, the consequences of this phenomenon are of great importance. It results inter alia in women surviving their partners by many years. It is also one of the major reasons for the increase in the number of elderly people. As the number of male and female births are approximately the same it follows that if the mortality rates of the sexes were also the same, the number of older women would be the same as that of older men. Thus, for example, if females in the past have had the same mortality as males the number of younger elderly in England and Wales in 1991 would have been .46 million less and that of the very elderly 1.12 million less (a reduction of 10 per cent and 31 per cent respectively) than the actual number prevailing (see Table 1). This would have resulted in considerably lower expenditure on income maintenance provisions, on health and social services and on housing.

It would incidentally also have increased the GNP per head in 1991 by about three per cent. This increase would partly have been genuine, the result of a diminution in the number of consumers without a reduction in the number of producers. However this increase would also partly be the result of a statistical convention that only goods and services which are sold are included in computing the GNP. The non remunerated services of older people are thus excluded as are the services of mothers and home makers while the services of home helps and mother's helps are included.

Major Causes of Decline in Mortality

The question of why the general mortality rate declined in this century is much easier to answer than the first question. The mortality of a population is determined by four factors: environment, behaviour, heredity and psycho social factors. The last two while of undoubted importance, are not strictly relevant to explaining the decline in mortality during the last nine decades. About the first two I have written previously:

> Amongst environmental determinants of health the three most important are: first, standards of living, including housing, nutrition, income and poverty; second, public health provisions and regulations, especially cleanliness of air and water, sewerage, refuse disposal, pest control, and inspection of premises where food is prepared, stored and sold; and third, working conditions, including length of working day and holidays, physical and mental strain, safety, contact with toxic substances and levels of radiation and noise. Behaviour which influences health includes drug abuse, smoking of tobacco, excessive consumption of food (especially certain types of food) and of alcohol, contraception, promiscuity, lack of exercise, lack of personal cleanliness and careless and reckless driving (Kaim-Caudle, 1985, p.150).

In all the environmental determinants mentioned there have been great improvements in this century. These are well known and require no discussion. The record of behaviour relevant to health and mortality is rather mixed. It seems probable that smoking and promiscuity are more common today than early in the century. Lack of exercise (including physical work) is also likely to have increased as a contributor to poor health and mortality. Important changes which have reduced mortality were wider use of more efficacious contraceptive devices and greatly increased personal cleanliness.

Individual, in contrast to public, health services have not made a major contribution to the reduction of mortality of the population below the age of 65 years. This has been convincingly argued and demonstrated in the writing of Thomas McKeown (1979) and is now the conventional wisdom. This view is well expressed in the 1976 Report of the DHSS Resource Allocation Working Party: 'We recognise that the prevalence of many of the conditions which are among the main causes of mortality is probably not significantly influenced by the intervention of health care services' (Department of Health and Social Security, 1976, para.6.31).

Health services, though their effect on mortality may have been marginal, have however greatly contributed to ameliorating pain and suffering, rehabilitating people suffering from disabilities and reducing the length of illnesses.

The number of the elderly and their proportion of the total population is influenced, as has already been shown, by the increased expectation of life at the age of 65 years (the reduced mortality of the elderly) and the increased survival at ages up to 65 years (the reduced mortality at ages below 65 years). It is also influenced by fertility (the average number of children borne by women).

Effect of Fertility on Size and Age Composition of Population

The importance of fertility can best be illustrated by an example. This is based on four assumptions:

1. 100 men aged 20 years marry 100 women aged 20 years in the year 2000.
2. They and all their descendants have all their children by the time they are 25 years old.
3. Their descendants marry each other.
4. Zero mortality up to the age of 80 years.

Table 3 shows the age distribution and size of three populations in which the average number of children of a woman is one, two or four respectively. Sixty years after the couples married in 2,000 they have great-grandchildren who

Table 3
Effect of average no. of children per woman on age distribution and size of population (zero mortality)

| Year | Event | Ages in 2060 years | Population Average no. of children | | | | | |
| | | | One | | Two | | Four | |
			No	%	No	%	No	%
2000	Couples marrying	80	200	53	200	25	200	7
2005	Birth of children	55	100	27	200	25	400	13
2030	Birth of grandchildren	30	50	13	200	25	800	27
2055	Birth of great-grandchildren	5	25	7	200	25	1600	53
Total population in 2060			375	100	800	100	3000	100

Table 4
Effect of average no. of children per woman on age distribution and size of population: based on German survivor rates 1986-1988

| Year | Ages of couples in 2060 | Survivor rate in 2060 % | Population Average no. of children | | | | | | | | |
| | | | One | | | Two | | | Four | | |
			No.	survivors	%	No.	survivors	%	No.	survivors	%
2000	80	45	200	90	36	200	90	14	200	90	3
2205	55	92	100	92	36	200	184	28	400	368	13
2030	30	98	49	48	19	196	192	29	784	768	28
2055	5*	99	24	24	9	192	190	29	1537	1522	55
Total population in 2060			254		100	656		100	2748		100

*children

Table 5

Effect of average no. of children per woman on age distribution and size of population: based on German survivor rates 1901-1910

Year	Ages of couples in 2060	Survivor rate in 2060 %	One No.	One survivors	One %	Two No.	Two survivors	Two %	Four No.	Four survivors	Four %
				Population Average no. of children							
2000	80	14	200	28	25	200	28	9	200	28	2
2005	55	53	100	53	46	200	106	35	400	212	17
2030	30	68	35	24	21	140	95	31	560	381	31
2055	5*	76	12	9	8	98	74	24	784	596	49
Total population in 2060			114	100		303	100		1217	100	

* children

Notes for Table 4 and 5

1. Both Tables incorporate the assumptions set out above except that zero mortality rate is replaced by the survivor rates of 1986-1988 and 1901-1910 respectively.
2. The mortality between ages 20 and 25 years of the couples marrying in 2000 is too small to show.
3. The mortality of the children and grandchildren (lines 2 and 3) before they attain the age of 25 years is 2 per cent in Table 4 and 30 per cent in Table 5.
4. Ages of Couples in 2060. Couples marrying in 2000 aged 20 years will be 80 years in 2060 and their children born in 2005 will be 55 years.
5. Survivor Rates. Amongst the 200 men and women who married in 2000 the proportion surviving until 2060 will be 45 per cent on 1986-1988 survivor rates and 14 per cent on 1901-1910 rates. The proportion of their children born in 2005 who will survive to 2060 will be 92 per cent and 53 per cent respectively.
6. The number of the population (Cols. 4, 7 and 10) for all three fertility groups in 2000 is 200. In 2005 the number of children born will be 100 for the one child group and 400 for the four child group. In 2030 the number of children born, allowing for the mortality of their parents before the age of 25 years (see Note 3) will be 49 for the one child group and 784 for the four child group in Table 4 and 35 and 560 respectively in Table 5.

are five years old. At that time these couples now 80 years old, make up 53 per cent of the population in which women on average have one child and seven per cent of the population in which women on average have four children. Great-grandchildren in the first population make up seven per cent of the population and in the second 53 per cent. In this sixty year period total numbers in the one child population had not quite doubled (200-375) while those in the four child population had increased fifteen fold (200-3,000). On the zero mortality assumption differences in fertility, even over fairly short periods result in great variation in both size of population and age distribution. The smaller the average number of children, the larger is the proportion of elderly in the population.

The assumption of zero mortality is replaced in Tables 4 and 5 by applying the survivor rates for Germany of 1901/10 and 1986/8 respectively (Statistisches Bundesamt, 1992, p.81, Table 3.30). These show lower aggregate populations for both periods and all three groups. The lower survivor rates in 1901/10 as compared with 1986/8 explain both the lower aggregate population and the lower population aged 80 years. The figures in the tables do of course reflect all the assumptions made and variations of the assumptions would result in different figures. The tables do however illustrate that fertility is a major determinant of both the size and age distribution of a population. At all levels of fertility the lower the survival rate (or the greater the mortality rate) the smaller is the total population and the lower is the proportion of the elderly. On the assumptions made, the effect of fertility on population size and age distribution is greater than the effect of mortality. Thus in Table 4 (based on 1986/8 survivor rates) the total population in 2060 for the four child group is 2,748; more than ten times as great as the 254 for the one child group. In contrast the population for the four child group in Table 3 (based on zero mortality) is 3,000; only 9 per cent greater than the 2,748 in Table 4 (based on 1986/88 survivor rates) and 147 per cent greater than the 1,217 in Table 5 (based on the 1901/10 survivor rates).

As the current mortality rates in England and Wales are already very low, the future size and age distribution of the population of working age will be mainly determined by fertility and only marginally by any further reduction in mortality. An increase in mortality seems at present unlikely and would be a reversal of the trend prevailing for the last hundred years. The number of elderly over the next 30 years will be determined by mortality at ages over 65 years and the number of births some 65 years to 100 years ago. An increase in the proportion of the population attaining the age of 65 years will be less important than it has been between 1901 and 1991.

The best measure of assessing current changes in fertility is the Total Period Fertility Rate (TPFR). This rate for a given year represents the average number of children that would have been born to a group of women who experienced the age specific fertility rates of that year throughout their child-bearing years, or expressed differently it is for a given year the sum of the age specific fertility rates of women at every age between 15 and 45 years divided by 1000. It is a more sensitive measure than the crude fertility rate which expresses births as a proportion of the total population or the general fertility rate which expresses births as a proportion of women age 15-45 years. Both these rates have the disadvantage of varying with the age composition of their respective populations. It is of interest to note that the TPFR in 1901 was estimated by the Registrar General to have been 3.5 already well below the rate of 4.6 which was estimated to have prevailed for the years between 1841 and 1881. It declined during the first four decades of this century to a nadir of 1.7 in 1941, obtained a peak of 2.9 in 1966 and has been well below the population replacement level of 2.1 (at current mortality rates) since 1980.

The TPFR is however not appropriate for measuring population growth at all times as it does not allow for the effect of female mortality before and during child-bearing age. This is a matter of crucial importance when measuring the effect of fertility on population changes in the 19th and the 20th century. In 1901 about 26 out of every 100 girls born had died before the age of 15 years and a further 13 had died by the age of 45 years. In 1991, only one in 100 died before 15 years and only a further two by the age of 45 years. Thus with the present low mortality rates the TPFR is appropriate for measuring the extent to which a population replaces itself, while in the past when mortality at younger ages was much higher the TPFR was not appropriate for that purpose. This requires a measure which allows for mortality up to the end of child-bearing age.

Summary

To sum up, the number of older people has increased mainly due to a steep reduction in mortality at all ages below 65 years and especially at ages below ten years. In 1901 only 87 per cent of females survived to their first birthday, the same proportion as survived in 1991 to their 65th birthday. Longevity after the age of 65 years was a relatively minor factor. The relative importance of the factors which contributed to the decline in mortality can not be ascertained, but in recent decades individual health services benefited the older more than the younger age group. There is no satisfactory explanation for the steeper reduction in female than in male mortality which occurred in all Western countries during the last 90 years. The future size and age composition of the working population will mainly be determined by fertility and only to a lesser extent by mortality.

References

Case, R.A.M. et al, (1970) *Serial Abridged Life Tables, England and Wales 1841-1960*. London: Chester Beatty Research Institute, Royal Cancer Hospital.

Department of Health and Social Security (1976) *Report of the DHSS Resource Allocation Working Party*. London: HMSO.

Kaim-Caudle, P. (1985) 'Health issues' in R.A. Chapman (ed.) *Public Policy Studies: The North East of England*. Edinburgh: Edinburgh University Press.

McKeown, T. (1979) *The Role of Medicine: Dream, Mirage or Nemesis*. Oxford: Blackwells.

Statistisches Bundesamt (1992) *Statistisches Jahrbuch 1992 für die Bundesrepublik Deutschland*. Wiesbaden.

Economic aspects
of an ageing population

BARRY THOMAS

Introduction

There are several economic implications of an ageing population. Some of the more important are examined in this chapter. No attempt is made to provide a comprehensive or detailed review of all the issues - space limitations prevent that - but a broad brush account to indicate some of the principal arguments is presented. In Section II some aspects of income levels are described. Various labour market consequences are considered in Section III, some effects on spending are noted in Section IV, and in Section V pensions are discussed. Section VI provides a brief conclusion. Statistical evidence on the changing age structure of society and the growth in the number of older people is provided elsewhere in this volume.

Income Levels and Inequality

Older people, on average, have lower disposable incomes than other members of society. This is the case in the UK at least as indicated by the first two columns of Table 1 which show differences between incomes of the elderly and average income levels[1] Interestingly, this is much less the case in other countries such as the USA and Israel. The distribution of income among older people tends however to be more equal in the UK than in many other countries including the USA and Israel, though it is markedly less than Sweden and Norway. This is shown by the Gini coefficients in columns 4 and 5 of Table 1. (A larger Gini coefficient indicates greater inequality in the distribution of income[2].) Differences in the degree of inequality across countries should not however mask the important point that in almost all countries a growing number of pensioners have incomes well above the national average

Table 1

National differences in disposable income, inequality and poverty 1980[a]

	Income, inequality and poverty according to age								
Country	Disposable income in relation to national mean[b]			Inequality[c]			Poverty rates[d]		
	65-74	75+	All ages	65-74	75+	All ages	65-74	75+	All ages
Canada	0.94	0.81	1.00	0.309	0.291	0.299	11.2	12.1	12.1
W Germany	0.84	0.77	1.00	0.298	0.340	0.355	12.2	15.2	7.2
Israel	0.92	0.96	1.00	0.360	0.429	0.333	22.6	27.1	14.5
Norway	1.01	0.79	1.00	0.250	0.229	0.243	2.7	7.3	4.8
Sweden	0.96	0.78	1.00	0.143	0.126	0.205	0.0	0.0	5.0
UK	0.76	0.67	1.00	0.266	0.240	0.273	16.2	22.0	8.8
USA	0.99	0.84	1.00	0.342	0.355	0.326	17.8	25.5	16.9
Mean	*0.92*	*0.80*	*-*	*0.281*	*0.287*	*0.291*	*11.9*	*15.6*	*9.9*
SD	*0.08*	*0.08*	*-*	*0.067*	*0.092*	*0.050*	*7.5*	*9.2*	*4.4*

Notes:

a *The dates for different countries varied from 1979 to 1981. See Hedstrom and Ringen (1987) p. 228 for details.*

b *Disposable income (adjusted for family size) as a proportion of the national mean for the total population.*

c *Gini coefficients for distribution of adjusted disposable income within age groups and for total population.*

d *Poverty rate defined as percentage of persons in families with adjusted disposable income below half of the median for all families in the population.*

Source: Hedström and Ringen (1987), Tables 4, 5 and 6.

income. The poverty rate, as shown in Table 1, is relatively high in the UK and in the US and Israel, but the explanation is different in each case: in the case of the UK it is more attributable to the relatively low incomes of the elderly, whereas in the USA and Israel it is more attributable to the greater inequality.

These differences across countries are sufficient to show that it can be misleading to make emphatic generalisations about the income position of the elderly in different countries.

There are however some features which are common to most societies. An obvious one is that the sources of income of the elderly are predominantly pensions and transfer payments (often well over 80 per cent of income) and income from employment is typically less than 10 per cent.

One important question is whether old age is a direct cause of poverty, and there seems some agreement that it is not age per se (with associated characteristics of frailty and failing abilities) which is a cause of poverty, but rather the dependency status of the aged. Social policies on retirement and pensions have often created or maintained a dependency status.

One assumption that is often made is that many elderly people are 'housing rich and cash poor'. That is, they may own a substantial asset, their house, but have a very low current income. The puzzle, if that is the case, is why more do not use reverse mortgage. This may be because there are substantial transaction and psychic costs, or perhaps simply because they are in fact not 'overinvested' in houses.

Labour Market Effects

There are likely to be several labour market effects of any ageing population. The most significant is that there will be a decrease in the supply of labour other things being equal. There may also be effects on the demand for labour.

The fall in the supply of labour occurs because labour force participation rates (that is, the percentage of a given age group in work or seeking work) are lower for older workers. This is evident from Table 2: workers aged 65 years and over have much lower participation rates than the all-age average. Furthermore, there has been a marked fall in the participation rates for workers aged between 60-64 years. These two features, which are common to most OECD countries[3] require explanation.

A powerful influence on the participation decision is the existence of compulsory retirement ages in most occupations and the fact that eligibility for some social security benefits is often conditional on restricted earnings.

This does not however provide a complete explanation. (It does not for example explain why many people choose to retire 'early', i.e. before the compulsory age, and why participation rates for workers who are older - though less than the minimum

Table 2
UK labour force participation rates by age 1991

	16-24	25-34	35-44	45-59	60-64	65 and over	All aged 16 and over
Male	80.4	93.8	94.6	87.6	54.3	8.4	73.8
Females	70.7	76.3	81.3	67.7	25.9	2.8	54.9

Source: Social Trends 1993, *Table 4.5.*

retirement age - are also lower). There does however seem to be a straightforward explanation in terms of income effects. In addition to the loss of employment income because of compulsory retirement which has already been mentioned there is also the growth of private pension plans which provide non-wage income and thus lower participation rates. Finally, if deterioration in health or diminished energy cause any reduction in the productivity of older workers then the wage offered may fall and this would adversely affect labour supply. There may also be demand side influences on the employment of older workers. Mallier and Shafto (1991) for example found that many men wanted to escape from their pre-retirement employment but did not want to stop working. They were particularly eager to return to part-time work. In many cases this was, according to Mallier and Shafto, because of financial pressure - large numbers of people who take early retirement miscalculate their financial position.

Employment of older workers can be crucially affected by employers' attitudes. In many cases there is resistance to employing older workers. A recent survey by the Institute of Manpower Studies, in which employers were asked what factors discouraged the recruitment of older workers, found that a third or more identified each of the following factors as important:

1. Lack of appropriate skills: this was seen as a major barrier with almost 60 per cent of survey firms claiming it was important or very important. It is worth noting however that this 'skills gap' is not peculiar to older workers.[4] Moreover if employers believe that older workers are resistant to change, they may discriminate

against them in providing training opportunities. This may lead to the confirmation of their beliefs and an informational equilibrium[5] arises which persists, but may not be optimal from society's point of view.

2. Shortage of older job applicants: the possible reasons for a reduction in the supply of older workers have already been briefly noted.

3. Lack of qualifications: this can be a barrier for older workers with the growth of credentialism - the so called 'diploma disease' - in which formal qualifications are seen as a prerequisite for entry to a job. Older workers who may not possess such formal qualifications, but who may have valuable experience which is a substitute, would thus not compete well with younger workers.

4. Pay-back period on training: when faced with two equally unskilled candidates (one young, one old), firms may reject the older worker on the grounds that the pay-back period on training favours the young worker. Obviously a 25 year old employee has a 40 year potential whereas a 50 year old has only 15 years. Older people do however have a lower level of turnover than younger workers[6] so training or retraining of older workers may be justified because of the greater likelihood of their staying with the organisation. Nevertheless, employers' assumptions about negative rates of return to investment in human capital for older workers can lead to the imposition of maximum recruitment ages for some jobs. These widely held perceptions mitigate against the employment of older workers, though the IMS survey showed that there were some firms (usually larger ones) which regarded 'ability' (for certain posts) and 'reliability' as two important factors encouraging them to look towards older workers, especially to meet labour shortage problems.

The level and composition of spending

The level of aggregate consumption spending partly depends on how much people save. Since older people typically have lower incomes, a rise in the proportion of older people may cause savings to fall (which could impair the rate of economic growth, because there are fewer savings to finance the flow of investment in new fixed capital formation). The evidence on this issue is however rather uncertain.

The effects on the composition of spending are more clear. It is obvious that consumption patterns differ across different age groups, for physiological and social reasons in addition to the different income levels. There will be an increased demand for the products favoured by older people and this will be especially the case in areas which have a higher than average proportion of older people. Most obvious in this respect is the demand for certain welfare services. This effect is compounded by other social changes, such as higher divorce rates and the rise of single-person households, which mean that the old are less likely to look after each other and will therefore be more dependent on state provision. The increase in demand for health services is perhaps the most prominent of the welfare services for which demand will increase though there are others such as domestic assistance, for example home helps, and pensions. As people move into their 80s they experience longer periods of permanent sickness. It is interesting to observe, however, that in the USA, experience suggests that it is the last year of life which is most costly in terms of health care and to some extent, with ageing, all that is happening is that this year is simply being put back. It might therefore be the case that the argument which says there will be increased health expenditure is exaggerated. This is especially so given that demand for some kinds of health care such as obstetric and paediatric services will fall.

The demand for institutional care will increase. There is a rising proportion of old people living in institutions or living alone. Part of this may be attributable to the children of old people, whose preferences are for nursing homes for the parents. It is beyond the scope of economics to comment on the social desirability of the outcomes of such preference, but if it is thought to be undesirable, the policy question is what economic or other incentives would be necessary to alter such behaviour.

Pensions

Public pension schemes are often characterised by defined benefits (related to final salary rather than being closely related to the income history of each individual) and they are usually financed on a pay-as-you-go basis. The essential idea is that pension finance is simply a current transfer from the working population to the retired population.

With an ageing population in which the ratio of workers to retired people is falling, there appears to be an obvious problem. In exchequer terms, as the number of pensioners grows a greater flow of contributions is required, but this has to come from a smaller number of workers. It is usually argued that a point will come when future generations of workers will not be prepared to take on the burden of pension financing.

It is clear that there will be problems, though the main issues are, as will be argued below, more complex than the simple situation just outlined. Public pension schemes are bound to be under pressure, even though they do not normally seek to assume full responsibility for pension provision. This is certainly the case in the UK. Mallier and Shafto (1992, p.34) note that the State pension was introduced specifically to alleviate poverty among the most elderly who could no longer work and who had not been able to provide any other form of income for themselves.[7] The subsequent history of state pensions shows many attempts to encourage private provision, and indeed there has been a substantial growth of occupational pension schemes, especially since the 1950s. In general the aim has been to avoid committing future taxpayers to an open-ended burden.

Similar problems with an ageing population arise in financing any care programmes, for example health, which are age-sensitive. The difficulties in these cases are however usually less acute than in the case of pensions.

There are several possible strategies which might be adopted to meet the problem of financing pensions. First, the level of current contributions to pensions, in the form of tax payments, might be raised. Secondly the rate of benefits might be reduced. Thirdly, the entitlement to benefit might be cut, for instance by later retirement. Fourthly, there is a range of other strategies which are designed to raise the number of contributors relative to dependent pensioners and thus overcome the effects of an ageing population. Finally, there may be possibilities for cutting costs in other areas of expenditure and transferring the resources to pensions.

These strategies will now be considered in a little more

detail. It is however worth noting at the outset that there are several different groups involved - taxpayers, beneficiaries, and various others - and the problem of financing pensions is thus a societal one, involving possible gains and losses for these various groups. A central issue concerns distributive justice in the transfers which take place across these groups. Some of these transfers involve inter-generational considerations in pay-as-you-go schemes: today's contributors are tomorrow's beneficiaries.

The first strategy of increasing current contributions poses certain tensions. Gillion (1991 p.121) notes that:

> ...growth in individual living standards, assumed to be shared equally between the employed and the dependent population, would fall substantially below the growth of real average earnings .. Incentives to tax avoidance and tax evasion would be increased and disincentives to work, at least in the formal, tax-paying sector, would be strengthened.

These latter points may require some switch from direct to indirect taxation in order to minimise these problems. If there were any increase in tax payments this would obviously limit other forms of social expenditure. There is an opportunity cost to preserving or enhancing pensions.

While the general argument presented here is valid it can be overstated. Net transfers from taxpayers to pensioners may be less than initially appears to be the case. Creedy (1992) points out that a characteristic of more recent pensioners is that they are on average better off than previous cohorts, because they have more access to private pension schemes and they have experienced much higher incomes in their working lives so they have been able to save. These richer pensioners share with workers the burden of financing poorer pensioners.[8]

The second strategy, reducing the benefit rates, would imply a decline in the incomes of pensioners relative to the rest of the population. There is a redistribution of income but not necessarily any absolute decline in real benefits of pensioners if there is economic growth.

The third strategy, increasing the retirement age (and age of entitlement to state pension), puts the burden of adjustment on older workers who were about to retire. This plan appears doubly advantageous in that it simultaneously reduces the number of retired dependants and increases the number of contributors. This does however fly in the face of the general trend towards earlier retirement. The question of what is the correct retirement age is discussed below.

The fourth set of strategies mentioned above for dealing with the problem of financing pensions comprises a range of possible measures to raise the number of contributors relative to the number of pensioners. This may be done for example by raising the labour force participation rates - any increase in the population in employment would raise the tax base. The most obvious possibilities here are for more women to be employed. There has of course been a substantial rise in female participation rates[9], so it would be simply reinforcing an existing trend. A similar effect could be achieved if there were a permanent reduction in the number of unemployed persons. Although the level of unemployment is likely to persist around the three million mark for much of the 1990s, the scope for increasing the employed labour force by unemployment reductions is less than from increasing the employment of women. Other possibilities are to accept an increased flow of migrants provided it could be ensured that these added more to employment and social security contributions than claimed in benefits. This is obviously a complex strategy:

The arithmetic of such a strategy is complicated and its implementation even more so, since it implies discrimination against the dependents [sic] of migrants and against those migrants who might themselves become dependent (Gillion 1991, p.110).

Another very long term possibility is to raise the birth rate though, again, this might be difficult and might raise its own train of problems.

The final strategy mentioned above is to achieve relative cost reductions and to switch expenditure away from other areas of public expenditure. (To some extent this may happen anyway with reductions in expenditure on, for example, infant and maternal health care.)

It is apparent from the foregoing discussion that the issues of pension finance are complex. The balance between contributors and dependent pensioners is sometimes seen in terms of demographic variables only, but it has been argued that other factors such as labour force participation rates, and the relative costs of other types of expenditure, are also relevant. Indeed the whole relationship between age and the labour market is not immutable.

One issue referred to earlier was the determination of the retirement age. It was noted that raising the age could ease the difficulties of pension finance, but individuals often choose to take retirement before the compulsory age. Given freedom to choose, individuals may be presumed to select their retirement age on the basis of maximising lifetime utility. This utility is a function of income and leisure (non-work). As real wages and private pensions and saving arrangements grow over time there will be an income effect. As people become better off they will 'buy' more leisure and this will lead to earlier retirement.[10]

The age fixed by the State for eligibility for state pensions is similar throughout Europe. It is typically 65 years for males. Mallier and Shafto (1992) argue that the choice of this age is mainly the result of historical accident and the tendency to follow precedent. This is no physiological evidence to suggest that workers suddenly become incompetent and ineffective at the age of 65. In any case, if physiological arguments were a key factor then presumably the retirement age should rise, given the improvements in the physical fitness of older workers over time.

In a few European countries, such as the UK, there are differences between men and women in the retirement ages relevant for State pensions, though the European Court has now ruled that there should be equality of treatment. This has profound implications for the finance of state pensions and it is understandable that there is much debate about what the common age should be. It is hardly surprising that the Treasury has favoured 65 for both men and women, the TUC has favoured 60. Other options are to specify a new age, say 63, or to have some arrangement with no fixed age. This is a major issue to be resolved, though space constraints prevent a full discussion here.

Conclusion

This chapter has dealt, in very general terms, with some of the economic aspects of an ageing population. It is clear from the previous discussions of selected Issues - the labour market, pensions, and consumption patterns - that there can be significant implications. This is especially so in the case of pensions where the use of pay-as-you-go schemes means that there is likely to be a growing financial strain unless some adjustments are made.

By way of a conclusion, we end with some brief remarks on whether such adjustments are in fact necessary and whether they can be made. Most commentators agree that some adjustments will have to be made though some play down the economic difficulties. Bond and Coleman (1990, p.249) for instance argue that 'resources have been available to overcome poverty in old age for at least the last 40 years, but the political will has not.' This statement is useful in identifying the importance of government initiative but it is somewhat misleading in its statement of resource availability.

Any adjustments which do take place will require conscious government strategies[11] and it is likely that they will need to be part of a wider programme of government social policies because, as shown in Section V above, there are many groups potentially involved in addition to pensioners. The issues are therefore, first the design of appropriate incentives for different groups to alter their behaviour or to modify their expectations, and second the distributive question of who should actually bear the burdens. The statement by Bond and Coleman misses a point of some importance in its assertion that resources have always been available. It seems to imply that support of pensioners could be almost a no cost process. This is emphatically not the case. All the developments which might be available to offset the consequences of an ageing population, would be available to increase incomes and welfare even if the ageing population did not exist. There is therefore a cost to be absorbed.

Fortunately, there is considerable time available. An ageing population is not something which appears suddenly and attempts to simulate the effects of different policies in different countries (see Gillion (1991)) do show various adjustments which could work. Somewhat paradoxically, however, countries which have the 'best' record in treating pensioners favourably are those, for example Germany, which might experience the greatest difficulties in meeting new challenges. This is because, having already made substantial efforts to treat pensioners favourably, there is less scope for further adjustments.

Notes

1. The figures in Table 1 are based on 1980 data, but the cross-country position has probably not changed markedly since then. The key features of Table 1 still hold, though the relative income position of older people in the UK may have deteriorated.
2. The Gini coefficient lies within the range 0 and 1. Perfect equality of income is represented by 0. For a technical explanation see Atkinson (1975)
3. See Mallier and Shafto (1991).
4. 51 per cent of employers in the survey felt that lack of skills was a factor accounting for all labour shortages.
5. See Spence (1974) for a seminal discussion of informational equilibrium.
6. Evidence on related issues such as employees' absence from work owing to sickness shows that the record for older workers is not markedly inferior to that of other workers. See *Social Trends* 1993, Table 4.19.
7. The 1908 Pension Act provided a non-contributory pension for those over 70 years with an income of less than £0.61p per week.
8. Furthermore, because pensions are usually included as part of taxable income, some of the pensions received by the richer pensioners will be clawed back.
9. For women aged 16 and over participation rates in the UK rose from 43.9 in 1971 to 52.5% in 1991) (The male rate was 73.8% in 1991). See *Social Trends* 1993 Table 4.5.
10. Sometimes pressures for earlier retirement may come from employers who wish to run down their labour force. For an interesting analysis of pensions as deferred compensation see Lazear. He shows that occupational pensions which are conditional on completed service may be a device for ensuring committed service, but a mandatory retirement age is imposed to prevent workers working 'too long', i.e. beyond the point

where the marginal product of labour (assumed to decline with age) no longer achieves the wage paid.

11. This chapter has taken for granted the importance of the government. It has been assumed that a socially acceptable fair provision of income support for all pensioners could not be provided entirely by the market because of various forms of market failure.

References

Atkinson, A.B. (1975) *The Economics of Inequality*. London: Oxford University Press.

Bond, J. and Coleman, P. (eds.) (1990) *Ageing in Society: An Introduction to Social Gerontology*. London: Sage.

Creedy, J. (1992) Financing Pensions in an Ageing Population.

Gillion, C. (1991) 'Ageing populations: spreading the costs'. *Journal of European Social Policy*, 1, pp.107-128.

Hedström, P. and Ringer, A. (1987) 'Age and income in contemporary society. A research note', *Journal of Social Policy*, 16, pp.227-239.

Lazear, E.P. (1990) 'Pensions and deferred benefits as strategic compensation' in D.J.B. Mitchell and M.A. Zaid (eds.)*The Economics of Human Resource Management*. Oxford: Blackwell.

Mallier, T. and Shafto, T. (1992) 'Options for retirement: mandatory or flexible?', *National Westminster Bank Quarterly Review*, November, pp.34-45.

Spence, A.M. (1974) *Market Signaling*. Cambridge, Mass.: Harvard University Press.

Is there a need for geriatric medicine? Does it do more harm than good?

MARGOT JEFFERYS

History of Geriatric Medicine

Since World War II, Britain, unlike most other technologically advanced societies, has developed a discrete specialty of geriatric medicine. Today, the wisdom of maintaining consultant posts in that specialty within the National Health Service is being questioned.

To understand the reasons for the present questioning of the desirability of continuing to make provision for the maintenance of geriatrics as a medical specialty, with its implications for training doctors as well as for the allocation of scarce resources within the hospital sector, it is necessary to examine its origins and its history to date. To do that, we must go back to the years before World War II.

Before 1939, the voluntary hospitals, particularly those in large towns which had medical schools integrally attached to them, sought to avoid the admission of those who were labelled 'chronic sick' or 'aged poor'. For various reasons, such patients were unwelcome. First, they blocked beds and were not 'good teaching material'; moreover, the illnesses which led to their admission were seen as intractable and chronic. The highly prestigious consultant doctors who, to further their lucrative private practice outside the hospital, gave their hospital services free, wished to be seen as concerned predominantly with aggressive interventions leading to cure. The chronic sick and aged poor, therefore, tended to end up in the huge wards of the old Poor Law Infirmaries, which, since 1929, had come under the control of the local authority Medical Officers of

Health. These could best be described by the metaphor 'warehouses', because the medical staffing was minimal and the pervading assumption was that old age implied chronicity, which required orderly nursing care above all.

The war years brought about some important changes in hospital-based medical work. The expected military casualties were many fewer than anticipated. Beds which were to receive them were, therefore, often left unoccupied: consultants from some of the best-known voluntary hospitals were redeployed, some to emergency medical facilities and some to the local authority municipal hospitals, where they encountered great numbers of elderly patients for the first time.

A few of those who thus found themselves responsible for the medical care of the chronic sick and aged poor began to question whether all their patients were inevitably bedridden and beyond discharge. Prominent among such people were Dr Marjorie Warren and Dr Lionel Cosin who became medical superintendents of municipal Hospitals. Sometimes against the wishes of well-intentioned nurses, who thought their regimes cruel, they instituted schemes for reactivating patients whose disabilities and incontinence they considered had been caused by, rather than been the cause of, their immobility.

In the years immediately following the war and in preparation for the introduction of the National Health Service, the Ministry of Health became aware of the success which they were having in their treatments and, more important, in the prevention of chronicity. The hereditary peer, Lord Amulree, at first a Medical Officer in the Ministry of Health and later a consultant at University College Hospital, London, encouraged other doctors to visit the pioneering institutions, and a Medical Society for the Care of the Elderly was formed to promote the provision of posts in a new specialty of geriatric medicine. It subsequently became the British Geriatric Society.

The newly formed Regional Hospital Boards were at first wary of creating new consultant posts in geriatric medicine, because the specialists in other branches of medicine and surgery were often opposed, seeing it as giving undue status and resources to erstwhile superintendents of the despised local authority hospitals, or likely to recruit to its ranks those who could not compete for the more popular specialties.

However, during the 1950s and early 1960s, much of the opposition from the elite of the specialists was worn down as it became clear that geriatricians who admitted older people directly to their wards could prevent their own beds from getting blocked. Additionally, at a time of considerable increase in health services resources, the geriatric specialty was not likely to be too competitive, in that its expansion was not likely to lead to too great a reallocation of resources, nor attract the brightest of the young medical graduates to its ranks.

By the mid-1960s, geriatrics was well established with consultant posts in all regions. By the mid-1970s, nearly all medical schools had set up Chairs in Geriatric Medicine or the Care of Older People. Undergraduate medical students generally were at least having their attention drawn to the medical care of older people. A new sub-specialty of psycho-geriatrics had begun and both it and geriatric medicine had been reasonably successful in securing training posts to support the consultancies. As a result of these changes and of the allocation of increased resources to the 'cinderella' services (which included services for older people) geriatricians were beginning to detect an improvement in the interest and quality of medical personnel applying for work in the specialty.

During the 1980s, although still a time of considerable uncertainty, geriatricians had developed multi-disciplinary teams which made a point of liaising closely with community-based service workers ranging from the general practitioners to the local authority social service departments and voluntary agencies concerned with the care of older, frail people.

The Negative Answer

Nevertheless, despite these apparently favourable outcomes from the investment in a medical service designed to cater specifically for the medical needs of older people, new or renewed doubts began to be expressed about the very existence of such a specialty. (This was a time when there was evidence that a lid was being put on health service expenditure and that in future there would be competition within medicine for scarce resources). The doubts have been expressed, moreover, by some of those who appear to have been most successful within the specialty as well as by others outside it, and this has led to a debate which is still continuing.

Is there a need for geriatric medicine?

What reasons are being given by those who want to see the discontinuance of posts in geriatric medicine, and, in their place, additional posts created in general medicine or other medical and surgical specialties, some of which might call for a special interest in older people?

Those who oppose the perpetuation of a geriatric medicine specialty have several reasons for so doing. First, they argue that age per se is a poor discriminator of medical needs. Some of those well over 75 years old have physiques and cognitive functions typically resembling those of people 20 years or more their junior, and vice versa. It is therefore arbitrary, as is sometimes done today, to allocate someone to the care of a hospital consultant purely on the basis of her or his age. (In some Districts, all patients of 75 or more are admitted to a bed under a geriatric consultant irrespective of their health needs).

Secondly, recent advances in the technology of medicine and surgery have brought it about that procedures which would have resulted in fatalities in very old people a few years ago can now be performed with impunity, resulting not only in added years of life, but an improvement in the quality of life. Older people should not be deprived of the opportunity to benefit from them.

Thirdly, older people constitute not only a rapidly increasing proportion of the total population, but an even greater proportion of those in need of medical intervention. In other words, medicine is increasingly about the treatment - curative, preventive and palliative - of older people. It would be wrong therefore for such treatment to be separated out from the main body of medicine.

Fourthly, experience suggests that most of those who qualify in medicine do not wish to work with a single age group, particularly if that age group consists of the very old. Most prefer an age mix, which would mean that they treated young, middle-aged and older adults. An age-mix would ensure that the research into diseases particularly affecting older people and the treatment needs of older people would not be hived off or neglected because the most scientifically able medical graduates were not attracted to work exclusively on their problems.

Fifthly, the very existence of special facilities for older people implies age discrimination in a society which is still prejudiced against older people, and where, therefore, ageism is insidiously present if not rampant. This is regrettable, but inevitable.

The Positive Answer

Let me turn now to the arguments of those who wish to see the specialty of geriatric medicine not only survive, but continue to expand.

The first argument is that it is precisely because older people are devalued by the rest of society (and frequently devalue themselves) that a civilised society needs to discriminate positively in their favour. It can do this by ensuring that adequate health resources are made available exclusively to them. In support of this, the contention is that the existence of geriatric medicine has ensured a greater allocation of resources to the medical care of older people than would have been the case without its presence. Before the war, the proportion of total national resources allocated to the care of older people was more derisory than it is at present.

Secondly, they believe that, if individual physicians and surgeons were to have mixed age case loads, the needs of younger people would inevitably be given priority in most instances. Insofar as resources are always short, rationing would operate informally, but systematically against the old.

Thirdly, proponents of a specialty claim that their detractors fail to understand the undoubted necessity of learning about the special physiological and pathological changes which occur in advanced old age, and about the appropriate interventions which are possible. The increasing likelihood that in old age, there will be a breakdown in many body systems presents particular problems of diagnosis and prescription which differ in essence from the profile of disease and illness in earlier life.

Fourthly, they point to the multi-professional teamwork, extending into the community, which caring for older people requires. It has taken decades to build up a cooperative pattern of work with other professional health and social welfare workers in and outside hospital. If the specialty were to disappear, the groundwork could face collapse.

Fifthly, they believe that the desire of some of their number to be known as general physicians or body system specialists rather than as geriatricians reflects their own perceptions of where power and prestige lie and not concern for the interests of older people.

Conclusions

Justice has possibly not been done to one or both the viewpoints which are now being expressed about the future of this specialty. This brief summary of the issues involved has, I hope, provided others who are equally concerned with the care of older people and the quality of their lives, with some of the background to the debate and with the arguments advanced by both sides, against which they can form their own judgements.

Ageing in France:
a policy of 'love thy neighbour'?

YVETTE MARIN

'Birth, Copulation and Death' was T.S. Eliot's summing-up of the life-cycle. Youth, maturity and old age are the more conventional divisions of life but should we not share Eliot's view that the only element cementing them together is the act of love: or - rather - loving, being loved and feeling lovable?

The proliferation of retirement clubs and societies throughout the Western world probably indicates not only that people are living longer but that they are frightened of doing so alone. The fear of growing old may be, partly at least, a fear of being rejected by society as no longer lovable. So, once free of paid employment, we continue to exhaust ourselves in multi-directional activity designed to prove to ourselves and others that our usefulness and vitality remain intact. Finally, we collapse - our heads as empty and our fears as vivid as ever.

In effect, we must live in the knowledge that we are ephemeral. Neither dizzying ourselves in a whirlwind of activity nor ignoring clock and calendar will rescue us from this. As Jean Cocteau put it 'Notre futur espéré ou redouté module notre présent '. (The vision of our own future, whether we welcome or shun it, shapes how we live today.) All policy-makers should memorise this quotation. Perhaps then we would create a world where old age could be accepted, respected - and loved.

Meanwhile, all through Western Europe, like modern-day Fausts, we sell our souls to any devil who promises to keep us young forever. Mineral water 'to keep our energy alive', mutilating surgery 'to remove the unsightly nodules of ageing fat', thermal baths 'to rekindle our desires' (loosely translated from advertisements in *Elle* and *Marie-Claire*) are amongst our constant efforts to remain eternal adolescents. Maturity is little valued and elders no longer revered. Old age is not considered a necessary experience in one's life - the summation of a personality - but the fate of a breed apart.

This paper will examine the situation of elderly people in one region of France and the success or otherwise of policies designed to meet their needs. It will do so against a backcloth of perspectives on older people themselves. To what extent have they fallen prey to an increasingly profit-driven consumer society? It appears that winners and losers can never be equal, even at the end of life.

Regional Government in France

The administrative divisions of France reflect the different stages in the country's history, superimposed one on another. More recent, incomplete moves towards decentralisation have further muddied the waters. The necessary links and co-operation between the different sub-divisions can tend to involve elements both of fiction and of friction. As later sections of this paper will show, it is frequently elderly people who suffer as a result.

Regions

The 22 regions of France were originally independent territories. The British have historical connections with one of these that is Aquitaine; this paper is concerned with Franche-Comté which is situated on the other side of France, bordering Switzerland. It is a small region in comparison to the others in France, representing only three per cent of the surface area of the country, or 16,188 square kilometres. At 1.08 million, its population is only two per cent that of the whole nation.

Besançon, with 126,187 inhabitants, is the regional capital. Prior to 1678, the date of the annexation of the province to France, Dôle was the capital town and the rivalry between the two lives on. For example, Besançon is a university town and Dôle is not, even though a University was founded in the latter in 1422.

Départements

Each region in France is divided into 'départements'. Regions now have decentralised local government but départements are still run - reflecting the imperial Roman model adopted by Napoleon - by a Prefect representing the State and named from Paris. France has 95 mainland départements, and others overseas such as Tahiti and the French West Indies.

The region of Franche-Comté is divided into four départements, each administered by a 'préfecture' and several 'sous-préfectures'. The four are Jura, Haute-Saône, Belfort and Doubs, whose préfecture is in Besançon.

Each département is further subdivided into 'cantons'. These are territorial divisions which have existed since 1775 but they have no budget. Nevertheless, since they equate with electoral constituencies, they contribute to the political 'colour' of the region.

Though linked into a region, and depending upon it for economic support, départements in general do not have much in common. Franche-Comté provides a good example of this. Each of the four départements of the region has its own characteristics. Belfort, with 131,999 inhabitants, is a city. Its two claims to fame are the fact that it was a fortified post designed by Vauban and its 103 days' resistance to the Germans in the Franco-Prussian war of 1870, remaining French when Alsace was handed to Germany. (Alsace became French again in 1918 with a cuisine and a brewing tradition to reflect its mixed heritage.) The Jura and Haute-Saône are both mountainous, rural areas with a sparse population declining still further as people move away to the towns.

In contrast with the other three départements, Doubs is far more densely populated, with Besançon accounting for 50 per cent of its people. Doubs used to be the heart of the watchmaking industry. This has given way to dynamic new manufacturing interests, such as microchip products which are exported all over the world. The Peugeot car factory, in Montbéliard, is the largest provincial manufacturer in France, employing 35,000 workers. Consequently, Doubs is far better off than the rest of the region and has distinctive political, economic and social agendas.

The rivalry between cantons, départements, regions, and towns - each with its own proud identity, each at odds with all the others - forms an interesting backdrop against which to search for rational social welfare policies.

The decision-makers

There are four of these: the Mayor, the 'Conseil Général', the regional council, and national government.

The Mayor is not a ceremonial official appointed on an annual basis as in Britain but heads the city council. His [sic] prestige will depend upon his popularity among the local inhabitants of the town. Hence some become national figures, like Chirac in Paris and Chaban-Delmas in Bordeaux. Besançon has had a socialist Mayor for the last 25 years in Robert Schwint.

A 'general council', with an elected president at its head, administers the region. The president in the region in question currently belongs to the Conservative Party (RPR). Within limits set by the State, he is free to pursue his own policies.

A regional council, again with its president, administers the département. Besançon Regional Council is also conservative controlled.

The State gives overall direction to all areas of policy and also funds them, in part. A 'Préfet', who is a nationally appointed State representative, is nominated every two years to serve a different town in France so that he cannot develop a bias towards the département he supervises. His primary task is to ensure that regional policies follow general guidelines dictated from Paris. Consequently, all decisions made by the Conseil Général must be approved by the Préfet.

The town, the region, the département, and the State each have their own budgets. Each is conscious of the impact of spending and fiscal policies on voters, and of the rising costs of welfare provision. Each of the lower levels depends to a considerable extent on State support, currently subject to sweeping cuts compounded by the success of the Right in the recent general election. Rising needs and falling funding, with in-built competition for resources, constitute a perfect vicious circle. Only the most utopian expect to be able to pursue the welfare policies they would ideally favour. Let us now see how this works out in practice.

Policies for Older People in Doubs

Every region of France has an ageing population. The Doubs area is typical. Its overall population grew by 1.86 per cent between 1982 and 1990 but, over the same period, the number of over-85s increased dramatically: by 48.74 per cent[1]. People do not normally seek outside help, however, until they experience some form of physical or mental infirmity. At that stage, they may turn to any of the various welfare providers: the town, the département, the region, or the State.

Whether by reason of a 'Latin' temperament or Catholic[2] individualism, people tend not to accept that they are in need of assistance until it becomes unavoidable; at that stage they frequently encounter a complete lack of information about services. Many manage by themselves, often in great distress and isolation, until their condition is bad enough to necessitate a hospital admission. Most families can tell a sad story about Grandad breaking a hip or Grandma getting confused and no one knowing what to do. The only thing their general practitioner could suggest was to give them the telephone number of a private ambulance company and the name of a hospital. In the course of my research, I asked many policy-makers why doctors are not better trained in advising people how to cope with dependent relatives. The question was received with a shrug: 'They are only doctors, you know'. (All direct quotes are translated from research interviews.)

Later, in desperation, when the consultant has said they can only keep the old person another week, or a month, or three months at the outside, the family is forced to rush around looking for an alternative. A few, who are lucky enough to know there should be services available, begin the search before the situation gets this bad. The kind of help or advice they receive, however, entirely depends on which organisation they approach because policies differ so radically between them.

Many families regard a social worker as someone who only deals with the destitute, prisoners or drug addicts. They would never dream of consulting one. If they do manage to refer themselves, or to be referred, it is the social worker who will decide what is the best solution for their elderly parent. A great deal depends, therefore, on the social worker's individual abilities. Being talked into entering a nursing home when you really wanted to stay in your own home can be a death sentence. With doctors doing too little and social workers doing too much, most people still tend to fall between the two. Adding to the confusion, are a range of social welfare organisations with differing eligibility criteria and varying charges. This may be better explained by means of examples, first from the city and then from regional council provision.

Practical Examples of Services for Elderly People
City council services: The CCAS (Centre Communal d'Action Sociale)

Each town or city in France is free to adopt its own welfare policies. In Besançon, with the population a curious mixture of upper middle-class and traditional working-class families, great attention has always been paid to this area of provision. 'Besançon' says the Director of the CCAS, Jean-Pierre Kerromen, 'is a leader in the field of social welfare, alongside Toulouse and Rennes, because of its wide-ranging services and ability to meet individual needs.'

The 'communal centre for social action' is a large body administered by the city council. It is chaired by the Mayor and has a governing board of fourteen elected members. Its office is situated in one of the most deprived areas of the town, and it is widely known locally for that reason if for no other. Its major forms of provision are:

1. domiciliary services to maintain elderly people in their own homes;
2. sheltered housing;
3. adapted flats for disabled people.

It is a moot point whether those who need this help can afford it, however.

Domiciliary services

A wide range of services can be provided to people in their own homes. First amongst these is usually a home help. Home helps are selected, trained, and supervised by the CCAS but this prices them beyond many people's reach. A charge of 73.97 francs per hour is made for those with incomes above the level of the State pension (the RMI or 'Revenu Minimum d'Insertion'; 'Minimum Guaranteed Income'), that is 3166 francs per month as of 1993, with a reduced rate for others. Since the minimum amount of help provided is two hours a day, five days a week, for many people the bill for cleaning alone would exceed their entire income. Cheaper help is, of course, available privately (typically around 40 francs an hour) but with no guarantee of standards. Other CCAS services include minor repairs to the house, or even complete renovation. An alarm can be installed, to summon help in the case of an accident, and severely disabled people can be maintained at home by a combination - for example - of night nurse, meals-on-wheels, adaptations, and personal care aides, provided that they can pay.

All services are means-tested and there is an argument that only those wealthy enough to buy the help they require, from whatever source, can afford to get what they need from the CCAS. The really wealthy have the greatest choice of all, culminating in the 'supervised flats' in major cities where the best services are offered by an establishment resembling a combined luxury hotel and private clinic. For those in serious need, despite the State pension, even basic help is priced out of reach and remaining in the community is not a viable option.

Sheltered housing

Local policy favours the construction of small units of sheltered housing, accommodating no more than 40 people. There are eligibility criteria which rule out the more seriously disabled. Once admitted, however, the wardens - who all hold nursing qualifications - pride themselves on caring for their residents to the very end, except in the most extreme circumstances. In reality, with minimal staffing levels, if two or three residents needed major help at the same time this policy would not be sustainable.

These sheltered housing complexes also stress how well they are integrated into the local community. In addition to their residential function, they operate informal day care for non-residents. Organised activities include bingo, dancing, concerts, outings. A particular emphasis is placed on good food, with daily menus set after consultation between the cooks, the residents, and the dietician. A four-course meal, with cheese *and* dessert, is served twice a day. On special culinary occasions, like Easter Sunday lunch, the courses expand to five with a different wine to accompany each and, in 1993, duck *à l'orange* as the main dish. Madame Lefranc, the warden (the French word is closer to 'manageress') of the Résidence Henri Huot says the only friction that ever occurs is about food. 'A good meal' she says 'makes people happy all day long, whatever their age or condition.'

But, visiting the place, I found the bedrooms small and the bathroom diminutive, albeit with a shower adapted for disabled people. Since residents bring their own furniture, social distinctions are clearly visible in furnishings and other belongings. These social barriers are also reflected in the groups people choose to mix with. Social workers admit that it is very difficult to place Black or non-Christian people there, since they would be rejected by the others. Even some of those who come in just for lunch are made to feel they do not belong. Furthermore, in 1991, the monthly cost of a room (with electricity, cleaning and laundry) was 2,550 francs for one person and 3,330 for a couple. Some receive a means-tested housing grant but they are still required to pay for meals and services at around 950 francs a month. Clearly, then, natural selection operates in these sheltered housing complexes, with a typical income there being in the 5,000 to 7,000 francs a month range. As mentioned above, the State pension is not far in excess of 3,000, with other benefits topping this up to around 3,600 francs. The poor are simply not advised to apply. In addition, there is currently at least a year's wait for a place.

The latest policy: adapted flats

Although specially-built flats for disabled people are of long standing in the UK, they are a new concept in France where the first legislation requiring public buildings to be accessible was passed only five years ago.

The Mayor of Besançon, not wanting to be left behind, is currently building brand new flats specially adapted for people in wheelchairs. Each unit is small, with thirteen two-room flats in a six-storey building. They are council-owned with council rents. Even so, to recoup the building costs, the monthly rent has been set at 3000F, closer to the average for a four-room non-adapted flat. Housing benefit (APL: Aide personnalisée au logement) may meet part of the cost.

The city faces reality: cuts and threats to service

Besançon is proud to head the annual French poll for quality of life. But the price is high. The townsfolk support only 30 per cent of the cost of local welfare policies and the rest has to be found elsewhere. Yet outside sources are drying up. 'Our problem', according to Jean-Pierre Kerromen, 'is the constant cuts in funding, set against constantly growing need. Inflation alone has increased our costs by ten per cent each year for the last five years'. He wonders how long they will be able to carry on:

> Previously, in France, we didn't believe in unpaid help but we are now asking people to establish self-help organisations to relieve some of the burden. We always believed the State should take care of its elderly citizens. Now, we are asking the next-door neighbour to help out. Our greatest strength was a highly trained and well supervised staff. We may not be able to afford it for much longer.

The dilemmas familiar from the British Welfare State now plague French minds. Is too much help cutting across personal initiative? How and where should limits be set? Monsieur Kerommen, interviewed in April 1993, answered:

> We are being reproached for delivering our meals-on-wheels to anyone who asks for them[3]. Perhaps some people are lazy and could cook for themselves, but they wouldn't ask unless they felt a need and we are answering that need. We serve 300 meals a day. One day, when we had a problem with our refrigeration system, we had to take a quick decision and serve only the most needy. We delivered only 90 meals that day and nobody complained. We could, of course, filter the applications but it is against our policy. We certainly won't be expanding because it is financially impossible, but we do hope to keep to the same number of meals. We need to employ 120 persons full time. We must pay them. If our finances are cut, our services will be cut.

Regional welfare policies

The next group of examples is taken from the regional administration.

Regional policies are not dissimilar, struggling for prestige and financial support. Since they draw on the same sources of support, Region and City fight it out to convince their funders that their welfare ideas and policies are the best. As they compete for money, votes, and power, each political grouping tries to offer something different, and to decry the others' policies as inferior.

Within the last decade, since services became decentralised, the Region has inherited the old nursing homes which previously belonged to the State. However historic in construction and venerable in tradition, these institutions carry a 'dinosaur' image which goes against everything the politicians and policy-makers are trying to achieve. Bellevaux, with eight centuries of history - during which time it has been at different stages a prison and a hospital for people suffering from venereal diseases - is one of them.

Bellevaux

Built as a monastery in the 12th century, Bellevaux is set in the heart of Besançon, by the river. It can take up to 250 residents; most rooms are shared by two, three or even four people and two dormitories have eleven beds each. The Director, Monsieur Michel, graduated from one of France's highly competitive élite colleges and was directly nominated for his post by the State. As a civil servant, he was at one time totally independent of the local authorities but, since 1986, has been accountable to both regional and national government. He currently feels under threat since one of the region's declared policies is 'to close all large nursing homes' (Conseil Général du Doubs, March 1993).

From the perspective of his career-long experience, Bellevaux's director denounces 'the fashionable waves in politics, which are nothing less than a showcase for power'. He adds that:

The fashion nowadays is for small units, yet the need for residential care has never been greater. Places like mine are in a financial strangle-hold and many have been forced to close down. And then what is there left to offer to the most vulnerable people? Here hey feel secure, they receive the best individual care, and everyone can afford to come here.'

The cost to residents, fixed by the State, is a daily charge of 216.80 francs but most of this is covered by social security, as it would be in hospital. It is therefore a cheap solution adopted by poorer people.

Monsieur Michel cannot change the physical structure of Bellevaux, with its beautiful 18th century chapel and its long inhospitable corridors. The only thing he can do, he says, is 'to become highly competitive in the quality of nursing care and staffing'. This is essential since the average age of residents continues to rise. The Director confirms that most new admissions are over 80; 43 in 1992 were aged over 90. Most are referred on from some other form of care, typically when they become too frail for sheltered housing or following a long hospitalisation. But Monsieur Michel becomes indignant if people describe his institution as 'a place to die'. His swift rejoinder is: 'You can die anywhere - your bedroom, your office, your tennis court. The point is that staying at home does not guarantee you the support you need in extreme dependence'.

The Director is at liberty to manage his home as he sees fit. The highly qualified staff receive the most up-to-the-minute training in geriatrics because Bellevaux itself operates as a teaching establishment. Like a specialist hospital, Bellevaux qualifies for the latest physiotherapy equipment. In a large gym, 200 metres square, elderly people are exercising under supervision. Next door, a jacuzzi is ready for bathers.

Is Bellevaux a bad place? Personally, I wouldn't want my own mother or father to be placed there because of the lack of privacy - or perhaps I am just being a snob. After all, although the residents come from the lower socio-economic classes, they do not seem unhappy. On each floor, residents eat together in small dining-rooms. Notice-boards display information about outings, arranged by an outside organisation. Some people seem lonely and lost, it is true. But those sad looks and depressive states of mind can be found anywhere. It may relieve *our* guilt to see an aged and invalid parent in a nice home in beautiful surroundings. We shrink at the sight of a shared room. But are we confusing our own perceptions with theirs ? Visiting a prim home in Alsace with flowered curtains and antique furniture, costing 10,000 francs a month, I was surprised to hear the majority of the residents complain of 'terrible loneliness'. Most are from high-income middle-class families and have always been strongly individualistic in outlook. The problem is that their children, satisfied that the home looks comfortable, hardly visit. 'It often happens' staff told me; 'once their parent is settled in, the family feel they have done enough and tend to forget to visit'.

Life is not like this at Bellevaux. One visitor told me his grandmother was happier there than she had been in her run-down farm, where she no longer had the energy to make a log-fire to keep herself warm. In Bellevaux, she felt comfortable, clean, and 'people are so kind'. Sharing a room with three others, she was never lonely; she also shared, she said, their visitors who always brought small presents for the four of them.

Nevertheless, any good word in favour of Bellevaux is impatiently brushed aside by Madame Dormoy, a local authority representative, as being at odds with the Region's latest initiatives to build smaller units.

Sheltered housing, regional style: homes are for living in

The new policy puts the accent on life rather than old age or death. 'We want to help people to live, not die' says Mme. Dormoy. The new homes are architect-designed: two-storeys high, each has 15 to 24 places separated into one- and two-bedroomed flats. A warden will make residents feel at home, in their own home, and they will be encouraged to bring in their own furniture. There is nothing particularly new in that. The innovation, according to the planners and policy makers, will be to 'help people help themselves'. Every resident will be asked to participate in daily activities, from peeling potatoes to playing bingo. The other aim is to prevent rural people from being uprooted when they are at their most dependent. The units will be decentralised and will give priority to people from the surrounding area, or with a son or daughter living nearby.

Is this 'a showcase for power', as M. Michel put it, or a genuine attempt at improving the conditions of dependent older people? It is, of course, too soon to judge. An interesting point to consider, though, is that elderly people from the rural areas and the smaller villages are generally less in need of help than others, being at the centre of strong networks of community support. If the Region finds it hard to fill these units, it may be tempted to open them to all comers. But will townspeople want to be uprooted to a life in the country?

One further advantage of these units is the minimal cost to the Region since they will be managed by a charity. This is exceptional. With a total lack of co-ordination, the authorities at national, regional and urban level - far from working hand in hand for the welfare of the elderly - typically compete with each other to spend more money with less results. One thing they all have in common is an emphasis on community care as the least costly solution. Is it a good solution for Besançon?

Community Care in Besançon

Growing older in Besançon, an ancient city, raises problems of getting about. The tortuous thoroughfares - with their missing or narrow pavements, steep gradients, and flights of steps from house to street - are the price older folk pay for living in and amongst historic houses. Some date as far back as the fifteenth, but most were built in the seventeenth and eighteenth centuries. Though architecturally protected, usually well maintained, and increasingly restored by State or private means, they are divided into flats which can only be reached via extremely steep staircases. Even a minor disability makes remaining in one's own home a real problem. And for anyone with restricted mobility, a fifth-floor flat can easily become a prison.

Despite the official policy at State, regional and city level, older people regard community care as far from paradise on earth. To pay for a daily help they economise on food and heating, to the detriment of their health. Living in an upstairs flat, or on a suburban estate off the transport routes, elderly people are stuck at home waiting for the rare moments of company they pay for in the shape of the home help. Most older people in Besançon have only a modest income. One lady told me she would refuse to the last to go into Bellevaux, unless she became demented and could no longer tell the difference. Sitting in her damp, smelly flat with no proper bathroom, she added 'I'm like my wallpaper: worn out, in tatters. I don't live, I barely survive'. Nonetheless, this is her home and she will not leave it. This woman has no home help, no meals-on-wheels - because she cannot afford them - and she will not countenance a social worker's visit in case she is 'forced to go into a nursing home and die there'.

Conclusion

Rather than competing for power by supporting opposing welfare policies, while at the same time trying to minimise expenditure, perhaps the authorities should try co-operation. One old lady, still in her own home, said:

> They all come at the same time - the district nurse, the home help, the meals-on-wheels. I'm rushed through my dinner or my bath and yet I spend the rest of the day totally isolated and

afraid. My bones are brittle, I constantly fall, what will happen if I hurt myself? I have an alarm and a telephone, but would I be able to reach them? What if I couldn't? Would I be on the floor for 24 hours until they all came back?

The Director at Bellevaux, advocating more co-ordinated services and a return to centralisation, firmly believes that: 'Scattering money around as they do now, most of it is wasted'. He sees ours as a materialist society where the old are consumers like everyone else: 'The more money they can afford to spend, the more help they get. That is all wrong'. Monsieur Michel's own vision is quite different. 'The last years of our lives should be classless. At the end, facing death, we are all equal. Shouldn't it be the time to remember that and act accordingly?'

Curiously, Mme. Dormoy, the regional official responsible for elderly persons' welfare, never once mentioned the elderly themselves. She spoke only in terms of buildings, investments and benefits. No doubt she is right that small, caring units are preferable to large ones. Nevertheless in Bellevaux, despite its unsuitable design, staff related to residents as people, and a real affection could be felt between them. In care for older people, would this not be a good moment to start thinking about them as individuals, setting aside professional views of what we consider to be their 'needs'? When I began my research, some five years ago now, I held firm convictions about the best policies for older people. I am far less certain now since I came to realise that each elderly person retains his or her own individuality and has been shaped and moulded by a unique history. The only thing they have in common is that they enjoy being useful, understood, listened to, loved. Are we able to guarantee them that? I seriously doubt it.

When frail and in need, we should all be able to choose freely from the widest possible range of options. These should be accessible to everyone, with no distinctions of class or wealth. This may be one measure of a society reconciling itself with ageing and death. If our elders were given back the respect they deserve - if they were no longer invisible in the cinema, in advertising, in fashion - perhaps our policy-makers would be able to replace the notion of 'care' with that of 'love'.

Notes

1 Figures quoted by Thevenet, A. (April 1992) in *Le Quatrième Age*, Collection 'Que sais-je?', PUF.
2 If we believe Max Weber's distinctions between Protestants and Catholics, as set out in *The Protestant Ethic and the Spirit of Capitalism*, London: George Allen & Unwin, first published 1930, second edition 1976.
3 Besançon is one of the front-runners in this regard. Meals cost from 25 to 50 francs, according to income.

Community care and user participation

LORNA WARREN

Introduction

When I was asked to give a talk on 'Implementing community care' in the European Year of Older People and Solidarity Between the Generations seminar series, I looked for a unifying idea linking these two titles. The most obvious theme, it seemed to me, was that of involvement or participation. One of the wider aims of this Year is to recognise the position and involvement of older people within society. The process implies challenging ageist beliefs and practices which attribute to elderly people a marginal status. In terms of recent community care policies a parallel course of action is purportedly taking place within local authorities which are now expected, through the system of care management, to identify users' needs and to give people a greater say in how they live their lives and which services they need to help them to do so (DoH, 1989).

This chapter critically explores the theme of involvement. It begins with a consideration of ageist stereotypes, both as they operate to exclude older people from mainstream society and in their influence upon the attitudes and actions of service providers. Current community care policy is then reviewed with a particular emphasis on its stated objective of increased user-involvement and with research examples to highlight the complexity of achieving this. Finally, suggestions are made for increasing the participation of older people in services

Ageist Attitudes

According to George Minois (1989) we can plot people's attitudes to older people in all societies along a continuum from 'contempt' to 'admiration'. Ellen Newton has described old age as 'a state of mind' the 'ruthless enemy' of which is 'convention not the biological clock' (Newton, 1980, p.27). If they are right, what are our own attitudes? Does ageist contempt or convention lurk beneath the surface of *our* enlightened exteriors?

Taking the media as a guide, the greatest ageism in our culture appears to be that of omission. Malcolm Johnson (1988) has asked why it is that in a society where nearly one fifth of the population is over retirement age, older people are virtually absent from our television screens? For example, they are rarely seen in adverts, unless selling traditional beer, bread or butterscotch sweets. When they *are* presented on the small screen, it is typically in stereotyped roles which emphasise the downside of age: misrepresenting all older people as poor, decrepit, sick, stupid, asexual and powerless. Alternately, they treat older people with condescending affection or hilarity - consider *Last of the Summer Wine* and *Dad's Army* (Midwinter, 1991). Malcolm Johnson believes that, while 'insulting distortions' are now more readily avoided than in the past apropos race, gender and disability, elders are still given short shrift.

Ageism Among Service Providers

Is it a different story outside the media or do we drag the influences of television, the press, books and other's attitudes into the work sphere with us and, if so, with what consequences? Such forces may help to produce, confirm or exacerbate ageist cultures within the work setting. Let us consider some examples.

1. Surrounded by people with perhaps the highest levels of need, it is easy for social and health care workers to lose sight of the general picture. While there exists a positive association between old age and the prevalence of ill-health and disability, it is worth bearing in mind that, even among those aged 75 plus only a small minority suffer from severe disablement (less than one fifth). Six per cent of all persons aged 65 and over suffer from some form of dementia. This figure rises to 22 per cent among those aged 80 plus (Family Policy Studies Centre, 1986), yet the majority of people (76 per cent) who are receiving

informal care suffer only from a physical disability (Family Policy Studies Centre, 1991) and may have purely practical needs.

2. The widely held belief - especially regarding older people - that mental illness is a permanent condition contributes to the limited availability of rehabilitation or therapy services.

3. There is a low value placed on receiving care and, in many instances, also on giving it. Attempts to resolve this mean that service provision is often underpinned by familial models of care which, inter alia, suggest the transgression of status differences (Warren, 1991). However, this ignores the benign forms of power inherent in familial relationships (McCourt-Penning, 1992).

4. I have recently been involved in evaluating a new initiative in social care provision in Sheffield. Neighbourhood Support Units (NSUs) were set up by Family and Community Services (F&CS) with the aim of breaking down the traditionally rigid division between domiciliary, day and residential care and replacing it with a more flexible and user-sensitive service (Warren and Walker, 1992). Supporting the need for change, a former social worker turned manager talked of the not so distant days when:

> ...people delivering services to the elderly were the bottom of the pile. You know 'If you want to take a break from childcare, get a job working with the elderly, it's a cushy number'. Still exists, still exists, and that is about the culture of elderly people being an area where 'Well, I mean, they don't make many demands and they're easily satisfied aren't they', you know. All you have to do is patronise them and they'll say 'Thank you very much, I don't deserve this.

Within the services, there thus exist the same or parallel stereotypes to the ones described earlier. At the extremes, older people are characterised as deferential or dotty: they gratefully and humbly accept any help which may be offered to them or they are beyond helping.

Social scientists have noted, moreover, how professionals attribute a great deal to these perceived characteristics of dependency and deviance: they explain the nature of the service via the nature of the users - or in this case 'clients' or 'patients' - using kinship and illness to articulate the social process. Yet the continuity of practices across a wide range of settings lends weight to the alternative view which sees the nature of the service as having much to do with workers' roles and being guided by institutional forms rather than being 'needs-led'. In other words, the 'patient/client' role is moulded to fit with the organisational culture, just as staff roles are shaped through training and cultural learning (McCourt-Penning, 1992).

Community Care Policy

The question is, can institutional forms and organisational cultures be transformed? Changes have taken place in UK social policy in recent years which call for more user-centred/sensitive services for older people. However, before their success can be measured, the reasons for their introduction must be considered. In the examination of community care policy which follows in this section, discussion is concentrated within the field of social care.

Community care, since the second world war, has been the key policy objective in the personal social services, pursued by successive governments. However, until the late 1970s, post-war consensus on community care existed largely at the level of political rhetoric. Characterised by ambiguity from the start, policy was never clearly and consistently defined and lacked the political determination and funding to implement it. In consequence there has emerged what Alan Walker first called in 1985 a growing 'care gap' between the need for care and the provision of local services to meet that need (Walker 1985).

Relating to older people, two main criticisms have arisen from this state of affairs (Walker, 1987). First, there is the longstanding critique of institutional forms of care based on the demonstrated relationship between institutionalisation and dependency (cf .Booth, 1985; Goffman, 1961; Townsend, 1962) and compounded by studies which show older people to be reluctant to contemplate residential care (Qureshi and Walker, 1990).

Second, the social services have faced increasing challenges from users who are unhappy with their bureaucratic organisation, complexity and lack of responsiveness to felt needs, for example through the growth of self-advocacy movements. At the wider level, the National Pensioners' Convention - formed by the TUC, presided over by Jack Jones and, with about one million members, the biggest pensioners' umbrella group - makes the influencing of government policy in public health and welfare provision the focus of 'grey politics'.

Academic studies have echoed these sentiments from Mayer and Timms (1970) onwards but, though they have undoubtedly had some influence, criticisms alone are not the cause of change in community care policy. Economic factors lie at the heart of the dramatic changes. In 1979, the first Thatcher government was elected and immediately began to pursue an overtly monetarist policy. Its chief concerns were with cost-containment and cost-effectiveness at a time when there was a growth in need occasioned by an expanding elderly population. Its desire was also to residualise the role of local authorities in service provision.

The interests of the government were reflected in the commissioning of Sir Roy Griffiths - a director of a flourishing supermarket chain - to review community care provision. His 1988 report, and the White Paper *Caring for People* which followed it in 1989, suggested a commitment to user-involvement. The four key components of community care were services that:

- respond flexibly and sensitively to the needs of individuals and their carers;
- that allow some choice for consumers;
- that intervene no more than is necessary to foster independence;
- that concentrate on those with the greatest needs (DoH, 1989, p.5).

When it came to service delivery, however, no practical guidelines were given for how the government's key objectives were to be combined with user-involvement. They were the development of domiciliary, day and respite services to enable people to live in their own homes; practical support for carers; case management; promotion of the independent sector; and value for money (DoH, 1989, p.5). In the discussion of these aims, use of the terms 'managers of packages of care', 'case managers', and 'caring for people' suggests that professional opinions will continue to dominate and that users will still be seen as passive recipients of care.

However, rather than being a model of empowerment based on clearly defined rights, user-involvement in social care is based on what Alan Walker refers to as 'supermarket-style consumerism' (1991).

Neighbourhood Support Units: A Case Study

In the light of the broader social policy backcloth described above, the response of one local authority to pressures for change within community care can now be considered. I turn, once more, to the example of the NSU initiative.

Neighbourhood Support Units were set up prior to the Griffiths Report (1988). The Report's emphasis on user-centredness was later made statutory by the enactment of the White Paper in 1990 as the NHS and Community Care Act. Nevertheless, the aims of the NSUs - to enable older people to remain in the community for as long as they so desire and to strengthen family, friendship and neighbourhood networks - were informed by the general trend within the social services in post-Seebohm years towards more flexible and user-oriented provisions (Warren and Walker, 1992). The NSUs were to act as a physical base for the services provided in the older person's home, as well as being a day centre and community resource.

Despite the goals of the scheme, evaluation of the NSU set up in the Manor area of Sheffield suggested that users had little, if any, say in the organisation of support. A survey of 67 older people using the new NSU services compared with 47 supported by the traditional home care (HC) service showed very little difference between the two groups. Taking into account those unable or unwilling to answer, roughly three-quarters of respondents in both groups said they had no say in either the quantity or the type of help received. The single most frequently given reason was that individual decisions were made by service providers:

They just give you what they think is essential. There's no frills (NSU).

There are too many chiefs and not enough Indians (NSU).

You get what they send and that's that (HC).

Some older people believed that staff in general were not really concerned about their welfare:

When you tell them what type of service you need they won't listen to you (HC).

One man commented sardonically:

They decide themselves. Well, perhaps to a certain degree. If I said don't come any more, they'd take notice of that (NSU).

A series of case studies was put together to explore in more detail the extent to which the aims of flexibility and user-centredness were met. They were based on the findings of formal and informal interviews with older people from eighteen households and their carers, supplemented by the interviewers' observations and user records.

A general analysis of need revealed a complex picture of often interlocking determinants. Older users' assessment of their needs depended on their individual perceptions of their health, the temporal nature of their illness or disability and on how these factors fitted with their varied personalities and life histories. They were also influenced by certain structural factors such as housing. While the norm of family care was still very much alive, there were pressures on family members - typically relating to paid employment and to the responsibilities of caring for others. This meant that the traditional hierarchical model of family care preferences (Qureshi and Walker, 1991) was rarely straightforwardly realised and, where it often came under considerable stress. In the absence of family care, neighbourly ties were activated - though support at this level was not as substantial and was often provided by people who were themselves over 65 years old.

Given the complexity of need, what implications did this raise for user-involvement?

The evaluation covered three aspects of NSU service organisation which were central to user-involvement. These were: assessment, provision/choice of services, and monitoring and reviewing of services.

1. Assessment

Examination of assessment tools revealed that questions about the needs of which older people spoke appeared on most assessment forms. However, the standard measures used to record information could not always capture the complexity or the challenge it posed to the normative value system underlying social care provision. The introduction by F&CS, half-way through the study, of a revised and supposedly more sensitive common assessment form tended to reduce the amount of information recorded. Response to the 15 page document suggested that (quality aside) quantity of information had an inverse relationship to the length of the form, largely as a result of the limitations on assessors' time.

On the other hand, the determinants of need listed above do not comprise an exhaustive list. Studies have revealed gaps between the received wisdom of professionals and policy-makers who devise, utilise and base their actions upon tools to measure need and the day-to-day experience of individuals (Percy-Smith and Sanderson, 1992).

However it was not simply that assessors, or 'team leaders', were operating within limited resources. They had no regulations or detailed guidelines on how to involve users in the process of assessment. There were no specific procedures or mechanisms to explain the process, nor to encourage or secure their participation. Users' views were certainly solicited, but how they were recorded or responded to lay very much in the hands of individual team leaders rather than being a joint process. Older people appeared unaware of the sections of the assessment forms set aside for recording their own views of what they needed. Indeed, some did not even know of the existence of the forms.

All the same, not all older people saw themselves as passive recipients of care:

> Well, I always have a say in what I get otherwise I wouldn't ask. It's important to stay in control, be independent. Once I lose that, I'd much prefer that I passed on.

However, this did not necessarily mean that they were active initiators of change.

2. *Provision / choice of services*

As for the 'packaging of care', there was evidence of a shift away from the domestic focus of the traditional service to meeting needs through new activities. These included the running of day centres by domiciliary workers, shopping trips, transport and laundry facilities, as well as more extensive personal care.

Yet the comments of older people and their carers showed that satisfaction with services was not always about the range of choice, but was also linked to the adequacy of help received within what was on offer. There is a risk of explaining people's lack of reference to areas of support lying outside current service provision solely in terms of the dominance of the traditional model of social care. This would serve to play down the importance to people's physical and emotional well-being of adequate domestic help. Older people also indicated how vital it was that flexibility did not compromise reliability and that the careful matching of users and workers mattered. Observational studies revealed the need for (further) expansion of support of a motivational nature, especially in regard to confused older people.

3. *Monitoring and reviewing of services*

Choice should not end at the point of assessment. Not only did users' circumstances change, with implications for their needs, but it was possible for older people to change their minds over time about the suitability of care. This is important to remember because a substantial number of older people come to the service in an emergency situation and are not always in a position to make decisions in those circumstances.

Evidence showed patterns of provision to be sensitive to new developments in need, though this was largely on the basis of how staff perceived those changes. Situations still arose where users and/or their carers had to make requests because of the lack of response from service providers. The expression of dissatisfaction was not made easy by lack of contact between users and team leaders. While the system of care management should in theory alter this situation, the creation of a new relationship between managers as purchasers and workers as frontline providers may remove the benefits of direct line-management.

In addition to the three processes which have been described, there existed a fourth means for user participation: the various user-group committees set up by the Unit. However, all the groups, the 'support services' user group included, tended to be dominated by younger people who were not housebound. Indeed, during the course of the evaluation, only one older person who received support worker assistance within her own home attended a user-group meeting. None of the case study sample appeared to know of the groups or their purpose. In the existing set-up, these groups were clearly not a route to wider user participation in the organisation.

Conclusion: Involving Older People

We are thus left with the question: what is the best route into participation?

The low attendance at user-group meetings was not really unexpected, given both the general frailty of older users of services and the well-documented tradition of poor attendance at public meetings unless they are organised around a 'burning issue'. People in general tend to adopt a passive stance in relation to the public policy-making process, especially if they are sceptical about the proposed 'pay off' (Percy-Smith and Sanderson, 1992, p.34).

Neither was it surprising as the model of user-involvement favoured by the government is a consumerist one which concentrates on the delivery of services as 'transaction'. In this model, older people are at risk of only being listened to if they have the resources (financial and other) to become 'customers'. Even then, control of services does not necessarily follow, since market forces and other 'externalities' are ignored. The model offers a 'pseudo-market' empowerment (Percy-Smith and Sanderson, 1992, p.49) in which services are still provider-led.

The fundamental requirement is to develop a 'culture of participation' whereby older people are more fully involved on a continuing basis in the process of service planning and development (Percy-Smith and Sanderson, 1992, p.34). Services must be user-led.

This is contingent upon the decentralisation of power within and from the statutory agencies. Suzy Croft and Peter Beresford (1990) argue that support and access are essential if participation is to be representative and a positive experience. Thus, a list of necessary ingredients includes:

- *listening to all users*: finding out their views using sensitive tools;
- *opening up organisations:* giving older people a more active role and access to records;
- *designing charters*: with rights of redress of complaints;
- *considering the how as well as the what of service provision:* including considering interaction at the front-line leve;
- *providing appropriate advice, information, training, advocacy and resources at all these levels.*

Such a model recognises older people as a community, yet one within which there may be specific groups with different experiences - black and/or Asian and white older people, for example. Indeed, black people are still more likely to experience the controlling rather than the supportive aspects of social services (Ahmad, 1990, p.32).

At the same time, the model breaks down hierarchical ranking between older people and other groups. The importance of social services to older people may thus be seen to be on a level with the importance of spare/leisure time activities to younger age groups. Neither is an 'objective truth; they are different perspectives based on different value-laden generational views. The aim should be to reconcile them where possible and to negotiate a consensus about problems and priorities (Percy-Smith and Sanderson, 1992).

Croft and Beresford believe that user-involvement is a practical proposition. The idea that it is not feasible now appears to be a minority view. Participation does not have to be all or nothing, but should develop flexible forms. Most older people do not want to be full-time participants. Participation does require resources but it can also lead to savings by making possible more sensitive, suitable and accessible services (Croft and Beresford, 1990).

Giving older people a voice and an active role in the health and welfare system is an aspect of the broader concern with ageist cultures, ageist structures and citizenship rights. Needs auditing can contribute to the empowerment of older people at intergenerational, local, national and - if work such as that conducted by the European Observatory on Older People (see chapter by Walker in this volume) is to be extended - even at international levels.

References

Ahmad, B. (1990) *Black Perspectives in Social Work*. Birmingham: Venture Press.

Booth, T. (1985) *Home Truths*, Aldershot, Gower.

Croft, S. and Beresford, P. (1989) 'User involvement, citizenship and social policy', *Critical Social Policy*, 26, 9(2), pp.5-18.

Croft, S. and Beresford, P. (1990) *From Paternalism to Participation: Involving People in Social Services*. London: Open Service Project and Joseph Rowntree Foundation.

Department of Health (1989) *Caring for People: Community Care in the Next Decade and Beyond*. White Paper, Cm.849. London: HMSO.

Family Policy Studies Centre (1991) *An Ageing Population*. London: Help the Aged.

Fisher, M. (1992) 'Partnership practice with clients with dementia' in *Social Work in Partnership*.Applied Social Studies, University of Bradford.

Goffman, E. (1961) *Asylums: Essays on the Social Situation of Mental Patients and Other Inmates*. London: Anchor Books.

Griffiths, R. (1988) *Community Care: An Agenda for Action*. London: HMSO.

Johnson, M. (1988) 'Never say die', *The Listener*, 119, 23 June, p.3068.

McCourt-Perring, C. (1992) 'The reproduction of institutional structures in the community', *Anthropology in Action*, 13, Autumn.

Mayer, J. and Timms, N. (1970) *The Client Speaks*. London: Routledge and Kegan Paul.

Midwinter, E. (1991) *Out of Focus: Old Age, the Press and Broadcasting,* London: Centre for Policy on Ageing in association with Help the Aged.

Minois, G. (1989) A *History of Old Age: from Antiquity to the*

Renaissance. Oxford: Basil Blackwell.

Percy-Smith, J. and Sanderson, I. (1992) *Understanding Local Needs*. London: Institute for Public Policy Research.

Qureshi, H. and Walker, A. (1989) *The Caring Relationship*. Basingstoke: Macmillan.

Townsend, P. (1962) *The Last Refuge*. London: Routledge and Kegan Paul.

Walker, A. (1985) *The Care Gap*. London: Local Government Information Unit.

Walker, A. (1991) 'Increasing user involvement in the social services' in T. Arie (ed.) *Recent Advances in Psychogeriatrics, 2*. Edinburgh: Churchill Livingstone.

Walker, A. and Warren, L. (1992) 'The care of frail older people in Britain - current policies and future prospects' in Olsen, L.K. (ed.) *The Graying of the World: Who Will Care for the Frail Elderly?*, Birmingham, New York: Haworth Press.

Warren, L. and Walker, A. (1992) 'Neighbourhood support units: a new approach to the social care of older people' in C. Victor and F. Laczko (eds.) *Social Policy and Older People*. Aldershot: Avebury.

Ageing in literature

ROGER TILL

In dealing with such a vast subject as literature, even in relation to ageing, I have been inevitably selective. My choices are personal and confined to a few English writers, starting with Shakespeare.

The best-known example of a pronouncement on age and ageing in his plays is the speech of Jaques in *As You Like It* on the seven ages of man. These lines are especially relevant:

> The sixth age shifts
> Into the lean and slipper'd pantaloon,
> With spectacles on nose and pouch on side,
> His youthful hose, well sav'd, a world too wide
> For his shrunk shank; and his big manly voice,
> Turning again toward childish treble, pipes
> And whistles in his sound. Last scene of all,
> That ends this strange eventful history,
> Is second childishness and mere oblivion;
> Sans teeth, sans eyes, sans taste, sans every thing.

There is no suggestion in this speech that there are any individual differences. Nor is there any guarantee of what would now be called 'solidarity between generations'. Moreover it would be a mistake to assume that these lines necessarily represent a statement of belief by their author. He simply put the words into the mouth of one of his characters at a certain point in a certain play. Strictly speaking it would be wrong to take any of Shakespeare's characters out of their context as though they were independent beings. The lives of characters in fiction or drama do not constitute 'case histories'. Even if the characters in a play or a novel were based on 'real life' models these figures of the author's imagination would be parts of an overall design in words, to be understood only in relation to other characters and situations. Admittedly there is a sense in which we may think of say Hamlet or Don Quixote existing in his own right. As long as we recognise that this could be only a very rough similarity to the original character no great harm would be done.

That being so, let us consider *King Lear*. This is a complex play and it would be facile to try to find in it any simple 'message' for older people now. With these reservations, however, we might think of Lear as an example of some aspects of ageing - to think of him as 'a very foolish, fond old man', absurdly stubborn, angry, and egotistical. After his youngest daughter, Cordelia, has infuriated him by her apparently lukewarm attitude when asked to declare her love for him, he divides her share of the kingdom between her two elder sisters and their respective husbands. Lear becomes more and more pitifully irrational, raging against his fate when Goneril and Regan refuse to make a home for him and his followers. It is true that his sufferings bring him new insights into the nature of human experience, even though he deteriorates both physically and mentally. During a lull in the storm there is a moment when he becomes perceptive and sympathetic about other people's misfortunes:

> Poor naked wretches, whereso'er you are,
> That bide the pelting of this pitiless storm
> How shall your houseless heads and unfed
>   sides,
> Your loop'd and window'd raggedness, defend
>   you
> From seasons such as these? O, I have ta'en
> Too little care of this.

Scholars differ about whether or not Lear recognises Cordelia before she dies. Whatever view is taken of that question there can be little doubt that Lear is at any rate partly responsible for the pain and anguish he experiences in the later stages of his long life. Ageing has brought him little happiness.

It is not only in tragedy that our literature provides examples of ageing. The world of Jane Austen's novel *Emma* is one of social comedy. The author tells us that Emma's father, Mr. Woodhouse, was a much older man than his years. He hated change and was preoccupied with his health. Jane

Austen writes, 'He loved to have the cloth laid, because it had been the fashion in his youth; but his conviction of suppers being very unwholesome made him rather sorry to see anything put on it.' We are told that 'he might constrain himself, while the ladies were comfortably clearing the nicer things, to say to one of the guests: 'Mrs. Bates, let me propose your venturing on one of these eggs. An egg boiled soft is not unwholesome.' That was quite a bold assertion for Mr. Woodhouse - who also approved of 'a basin of nice smooth gruel, thin, but not too thin.'

The life teeming through the pages of Dickens naturally included a number of older people. He himself never attained what we should regard as old age: he was fifty eight when he died - six years older than Shakespeare. Dickens appeared to be less interested in describing people at work than in writing about them in their leisure hours. He was conscious of the way younger members of the family looked after their elders - in days long before there were carers or home helps in the present sense of those words. Sometimes this care for older people went hand in hand with the pleasure that both generations took in eccentric hobbies. An example of that occurs in one of Dickens's finest novels, *Great Expectations*. Wemmick, who is confidential clerk to a lawyer named Jaggers, lives in a small wooden cottage, the top of which is cut out and painted like a battery mounted with guns. He has a flagstaff and on Sundays he runs up a flag. "At nine o'clock every night, Greenwich time,' said Wemmick,. 'the gun fires." A little later: "Well, it's a good thing, you know. It brushes the Newgate cobwebs away, and pleases the Aged. You wouldn't mind being at once introduced to the Aged, would you? It wouldn't put you out?"

Wemmick then introduces Pip, the narrator of the novel, to his father, whom Wemmick addresses as 'aged parent' - soon to be in great spirits. It may be that Dickens regarded this character not only as an individual but as a type - an embodiment of the later stages of life. Dickens certainly had a strong sense of continuity: the links between the generations. It is significant that his books were often read aloud to virtually the whole family - children and grandparents included.

Sometimes even a few words in a nineteenth century novel can be revealing on the subject of ageing - for instance, a single sentence in one of Trollope's Barsetshire novels, *Doctor Thorne*:

Doctor Thomas continues to extend his practice, to the great disgust of Dr. Fillgrave; and when Mary suggested to him that he should retire, he always boxed her ears.

George Eliot understood people of all ages. Perhaps the most subtle of her studies of an ageing person is that of Casaubon, the dried-up pedant married to a much younger woman in *Middlemarch* - but that very fine novel does not yield brief quotations that would do it justice. Whether through his own fault or circumstances beyond his control, Michael Henchard in *The Mayor of Casterbridge* failed to cope either with ageing or with personal and social relationships. This man - by occupation a hay-trusser - sells his wife and child for five guineas at a country fair when under the influence of drink. Later he makes good progress in a worldly sense, becoming the local mayor and a magistrate. Henchard then has a series of misfortunes both in business and in love. He deteriorates in almost every way, finally dying miserably alone. He had fallen out with the society that had helped to make him successful.

In some of his writings Hardy seemed to suggest that human beings are influenced not so much by their physical age and ageing as by the age in which they live - the social prejudices that prevent Jude from going to a university; the marriage laws of mid and late Victorian England; and the challenging views of Darwin and Huxley on the origin of humankind. All these factors may have contributed to making some people prematurely aged, incapable of fulfilling their earlier potential. Hardy was sensitively aware of these frustrations. His attitude might have been that it is not age or ageing that is the enemy: it is Fate, which traps human beings in its net.

Hardy lived to be eighty-seven. Unlike Yeats, who wrote in one of his poems, 'An aged man is but a paltry thing', he wrote regretfully about his continued power of feeling intensely in spite of his years. Here is a short poem of his on that subject:

> I look into my glass
> And view my wasting skin,
> And say, 'Would God it came to pass
> My heart had shrunk as thin!'

For then, I, undistrest
By hearts grown cold to me,
Could lonely wait my endless rest
With equanimity.

But Time, to make me grieve,
Part steals, lets part abide;
And shakes this fragile frame at eve
With throbbings of noontide.

People on the verge of retirement are often advised to cultivate interests and hobbies or to continue those they have already pursued in their spare time. Charles Lamb, the early nineteenth century essayist and dramatic critic, who worked in London as a clerk in the East India Office, had made abundant use of his leisure with his pen for many years before he retired was In his essay 'The Superannuated Man' ,Lamb describes his feelings at retirement. His health had declined. At the age of fifty, after thirty-five years in employment, he was given a pension to the amount of two-thirds of his accustomed salary - very good terms, it may be thought, and a contrast to the conditions endured by many people then.

About his retirement Lamb writes, 'For the first day or two I felt stunned, overwhelmed ... I wandered about, thinking I was happy, and knowing that I was not. It was like passing out of time into Eternity ... It seemed to me that I had more time on my hands than I could ever manage'. Then comes this warning: 'And here let me caution persons grown old in active business, not lightly, nor without weighing their own resources, to forego their customary employment all at once, for there may be danger in it'. After a week or two Lamb still missed his old chains, as he called them, in the counting-house. Near the end of his essay he writes, 'I have done all that I came into the world to do'. He retired in 1825 and lived ten more years. In spite of what he had written in his essay he did keep up some of his interests. Besides doing a great deal of reading he made a few new friends and sometimes walked a dozen miles a day into the country.

The use of leisure in retirement is relevant to some words written by George Orwell in his book *The Lion and the Unicorn*. Discussing characteristics of his fellow-countrymen, he emphasises 'the addiction to hobbies and spare-time occupations, the *privateness* of English life'. He writes:

We are a nation of flower-lovers, but also a nation of stamp-collectors, pigeon-fanciers, amateur carpenters, coupon-snippers, dart-players, crossword-puzzle fans. All the culture that is most truly native centres round things which even when they are communal are not official - the pub, the football match, the back garden, the fireside and the 'nice cup of tea'.

A humorous testimony to the value of preparation for the later years occurs in *Alice in Wonderland* - the verses recited by Alice to the Caterpillar recounting a conversation between a youth and his father. These are two of the verses:

'You are old,' said the youth, 'and your jaws are
    too weak
For anything tougher than suet;
Yet you finished the goose, with the bones and
    the beak -
Pray, how did you manage to do it?'

'In my youth,' said his father, 'I took to the law,
And argued each case with my wife;
And the muscular strength which it gave to my
    jaw,
Has lasted the rest of my life.

Lewis Carroll, who must have known that children are inclined to exaggerate the age of their elders, might have relished the opening of a book written in the earlier years of the present century: 'Mr. Salteena was an elderly man of 42 ...' Daisy Ashford, the author, was nine years old when she wrote that book. Yet it was not a child but a grown man - Lytton Strachey - who, in his biography of Queen Victoria, referred to the Prime Minister at the beginning of her reign - Lord Melbourne - as being 'now with old age upon him'. He was fifty-eight - but we should reflect that although some people lived to greater ages in the early and middle years of the nineteenth century, a person of fifty-eight was comparatively elderly.

Arnold Bennett's *The Old Wives' Tale*, published towards

the end of the reign of King Edward the Seventh, has much to say implicitly about ageing and the continuity of life. The two main characters are sisters living in the Potteries when the story begins. Sophia, the younger one, goes to Paris, married to a man who soon deserts her. Constance, the elder sister, remains all her life in the Five Towns (Bennett's name for the Potteries), marries, has a son, and is widowed. There is a moving scene when, after many years, Sophia comes back to England and meets her sister again. The book says much about youth, the older years, and the renewal of life in another generation.

Here are two short quotations. The first is about Sophia in Paris before her return to the Potteries. She has made a success in running a hotel. People regard her as a very wise woman. 'And yet', the author says, 'she had been guilty of the capital folly of cutting herself off from her family. She was ageing, and she was alone in the world.' It could be said that there was a lack of social participation.

The other quotation is more cheerful. Sophia is back in the Potteries talking to her sister:

> When the dogs dozed, the sisters began to look through photograph albums, of which Constance had several, bound in plush on morocco. Nothing will sharpen the memory, evoke the past, raise the dead, rejuvenate the ageing, and cause both sighs and smiles like a collection of photographs gathered together during long years of life.

The power of memory to bring back joyful occasions in earlier years is evoked imaginatively by Lytton Strachey in *Queen Victoria*. As the Queen lies dying at the end of her long life and her long reign she is pictured in these words:

> Perhaps her fading mind called up once more the shadows of the past to float before it, and retraced, for the last time, the vanished visions of that long history - passing back and back, through the cloud of years, to older and ever older memories - to the spring woods at Osborne, so full of primroses for Lord Beaconsfield - to Lord Palmerston's queer clothes and high demeanour, and Albert's face under the green lamp, and Albert's first stag at Balmoral, and Albert in his blue and

silver uniform, and the Baron coming in through a doorway, and Lord M. dreaming at Windsor with the rooks cawing in the elm-trees, and the Archbishop of Canterbury on his knees in the dawn, and the old King's turkey-cock ejaculations, and Uncle Leopold's soft voice at Claremont, and Lehzen with the globes, and her mother's feathers sweeping down towards her, and a great old repeater-watch of her father's in its tortoise-shell case, and a yellow rug, and some friendly flounces of sprigged muslin, and the trees and the grass at Kensington.

The character, experience of life, and sometimes religious beliefs of a creative writer may all be reflected in the way that the subject of ageing is treated. From an orthodox point of view Hardy was an unbeliever, though he longed to have the faith of his forbears, the faith in which he himself was nurtured. Browning had fewer misgivings. His poem 'Rabbi Ben Ezra' is based on a famous Jewish scholar of that name. The words given to the rabbi may well illustrate Browning's own response to age and ageing and gives us all food for thought:

> Grow old along with me!
> The best is yet to be,
> The last of life, for which the first was made:
> Our times are in his hand
> Who saith, 'A whole I planned,
> 'Youth shows but half; trust God;
> see all nor be afraid!'

Social participation and older people: the life stories of older women in a Durham ex-mining town

ROBIN HUMPHREY

Introduction

The social lives of older people is a subject that has received considerable academic attention (Wenger, 1984; Qureshi and Walker, 1989). The breadth and nature of older people's personal relationships with their family, their friends and their neighbours have been researched and surmised about to such an extent not only because they are intrinsically interesting, but also because it is believed that an understanding of older people's intimate and immediate lives can tell us, both about contemporary society, but also about the process of social change and also how people lived their lives in the past.

Among the unique possessions of older people are their memories of times that the rest of us can only read about. One frightening implication of the ever-forward march of time is that these memories are gradually being lost to us as, year by year, we lose our most elderly citizens. One deeply unfortunate consequence of this inevitable process is that, in the case of large sections of the population who benefited from only limited education and for whom writing was not a part of their cultural make-up, such reminiscences are all the first hand knowledge we have, and when they are no longer obtainable we are left, at best, with the assumptions and musings of writers who might never have had any contact with their subjects and, at worst, with nothing at all, a part of history irretrievably lost.

In this chapter, I shall explore briefly the findings of a research project into the social lives of older people which adopted a historical approach and which, as a consequence, employed a particular research method, the life story method, that sought to capture and preserve for posterity older people's memories of their lives. Much has been written about the appropriateness of this method for social science research, about the potential it offers and the pitfalls it may present (Bertaux, 1981; Plummer, 1990). Although there are dangers in relying on such a fallible resource as the human memory (Lummis, 1987), and although problems arise from the fact that life stories are, strictly, not biographies but products of the interaction between the interviewer and the interviewee (Gearing and Dant, 1990), I believe that this method can profitably be used for historical analysis, especially if the life stories are properly framed in their cultural context.

The Sociological Context

The main sociological debate to which this study relates is that concerning the impact of rapid social change on communities. The parameters for this debate were largely set by one of the classical sociologists, Ferdinand Toennies, who developed the concepts of *gemeinschaft* and *gesellschaft*, which can loosely be translated as 'community' and 'association', to distinguish between two types of society, one based on social relationships that were small-scale, personal and particular, the other on relationships that were large-scale, impersonal and more universal (Toennie,s 1957). *Gemeinschaft* societies were bound together by affective and traditional ties, where behaviour had a spontaneous nature, while *gesellschaft* societies were based upon individualism, contractualism and the rational pursuit of interest, and spurned behaviour that was more contrived than spontaneous. The former type of social bonding tended to operate in economically underdeveloped and more rurally-based societies, and the latter in modern, urbanised and industrial societies. Associated with this notion of a transition from *gemeinschaft* to *gesellschaft* is the proposition that the primary group will disintegrate and give way to an impersonal, rationalised, urban mass society.

Evidence from a series of studies carried out in the twentieth century casts doubt on the accuracy of Toennies's prediction (Young and Wilmott, 1957; Roberts, 1971; Dennis et al., 1976; Ross, 1983). From these studies it became evident that within urban settings there had developed neighbourhoods with strong informal ties and extended family networks through which self-help and mutual aid flourished. These were neighbourhoods where the urban working class lived, and they were characterised by powerful affective bonds between men and their workmates and between women and their kin and neighbours. These ties were never more powerful than in the traditional single-industry communities based on coal, steel or shipbuilding, where work and leisure, family and communal life were bound together, creating a 'high moral density' and reinforcing 'sentiments of belongingness to a work-dominated collectivity' (Lockwood, 1966, p.251).

Ferryhill, an ex-mining town in County Durham, where my own research took place, provides an ideal setting for a study of such a collectivity. The Dean and Chapter pit (so named because it was sunk on land owned by Durham Cathedral) was opened in 1905, at a time when the Great North coalfield in which it was situated was already in decline. Whereas previously Ferryhill had been surrounded by small mining settlements but had lacked a pit of its own, from this time on it was to grow into one of the biggest mining towns boasting one of the biggest coal mines in the area. The informants in this study had spent either all or the majority of their lives in Ferryhill (the most recent incomer had moved to the town 35 years prior to the research) and most had either worked at the local colliery or else were married to miners who had worked there. They were all therefore steeped in the distinctive culture surrounding the mining industry, a culture that is fast disappearing with the demise of the British coal industry.

Mining work is physically demanding and in the United Kingdom done exclusively by men, many of whom possess skills relevant or peculiar to the industry. For most of the miners in Ferryhill, the pit was only a short walk away from their colliery homes, and so groups of friends and neighbours would gather and walk to work as the time their shift was to begin approached. Work and leisure pursuits were closely linked, colleagues at work sharing their social lives together. Married women were rarely involved in paid employment, working instead in the home bringing up a family. The tradition of sons following their father into the pit was strong and intermarriage within the community common. The children of the mining family therefore often settled down close to their parents' home (hence the term 'family pit' (Beynon et al., 1991)), and continuity of work and support systems were established. Just as Young and Wilmott (1957) found in Bethnal Green in the working class East End of London, the relationship between mother and daughter was particularly strong, maternal help with the problems of starting and coping with a family being reciprocated by guarantees that, later on, mothers would be looked after as faculties declined in old age. The local community was bound together by the strongest of ties: work and family dominated life in a way rarely found outside the mining industry.

The closure of the pit in 1966, coupled with policies adopted by Durham County Council in response to a declining industrial base, brought about fundamental changes in these patterns of employment and lifestyle. First, the decline of mining as a source of employment has caused a sizeable proportion of the population, and in particular the young adults, to travel in search of work, sometimes to distant parts of the country (Taylor, 1966; House and Knight, 1967). Secondly, Ferryhill was transformed from a mining community into a working class commuter town. The number of jobs located there dwindled as it gradually became what was essentially a dormitory town for the factories planted in the trading estates established in nearby towns (Austrin and Beynon, 1981).

The Analysis of Life Stories

The life story interviews sought to explore the informants' memories of their part in the history of the town. The fieldwork was carried out during 1981 and 1982, and involved the screening of a randomly selected sample of people aged 60-75 from the age/sex register of the only GP's practice in the town in order to identify two groups at the extremes of social participation, the socially involved and the socially isolated. Ten informants from each group subsequently agreed to be interviewed about their life stories. The resultant life stories reflected the uniqueness of the individual life and the communality of a shared culture; the task was to develop an analysis that would explain, in Philip Abrams's famous phrase, 'the puzzle of human agency ... in terms of the process of social structuring' (Abrams, 1982, p.x).

One way in which the life stories were analysed was via what I have called a historical ethnography, that is, the description of a particular aspect of a culture as it changes over time (Humphrey, 1993b). Elsewhere, I have argued for an analysis of life stories that follows the individual over the life course, and for the development of the notion of a social career to aid such an analysis. This way of analysing life stories is particularly appropriate for identifying patterns of continuity and discontinuity in the individual lives of older people already identified as extremely socially involved or socially isolated (Humphrey, 1993a). Here, although I shall use the notion of a social career, I shall develop a rather different type of analysis, one which treats interviewees as ethnographic informants, the aim being to obtain accurate descriptions of the interviewees' life trajectories in social contexts (Bertaux and Kohli, 1984). The procedures I followed in constructing my analytic framework were similar to those elaborated by Strauss and Corbin (1990) for the generation of grounded theory: the life stories were separated into historical categories and then further classified by key concepts (such as 'Life in the Home' and 'Formal Social Activities'). These categories were systematically related to one another to produce the core category, or the story line, at the centre of the resultant narrative about the phenomenon under study, the transformation over the course of this century of women's social lives in a Durham mining community.

The most striking testimony of the life stories is that men and women have, throughout their lives, occupied completely different social spheres. This social divide, based on gender, had strong historical roots and was reinforced by traditional cultural norms and values which emphasised clear divisions of labour and leisure both inside and outside the home. The influence of gender is so pervasive that all the life stories are coloured by it. The following, however, will concentrate on the lives of the women informants, partly because of restrictions of space but also because it is in the stories of the women that the clearest illustrations may be found of the profound changes that have taken place in the nature of women's social experiences. Discussion of the social lives of the male informants will therefore be limited to the placing of the women's lives in their proper social context.

The early 1900s

Most children born into mining communities in the early part of this century belonged to large families. To have fewer than six brothers and sisters was unusual, and many children had ten or more. The men in mining communities commonly frequented the Workingmen's Club, where friendships created initially through working together in a hard and dangerous industry could be maintained in recreation. A large part of their lives were spent outside the home, and when they were at home, they were either eating or resting before another (up to ten-hour) shift at the pit. Their wives, on the other hand, spent almost all their time in the home and rarely ventured further than the street. Many informants made it clear that their mothers did not have a social life as they were too busy with the daily round of domestic chores and were taken up with the constant attention demanded by so many children. As the children grew up, the domestic burdens changed rather than diminished as the boys began their working lives down the pit and a different cycle of household responsibilities emerged; shift work meant that men were returning to the house at all times of the day requiring baths, clean clothes and food after their spell underground.

Neighbours were friendly and ready and willing to help in an emergency, but as a rule did not enter the house. When there was illness or some other problem which legitimately required neighbourly help, it was women rather than men who answered the call. Constraints of time and space did not permit much entertaining within the home. Most miners lived in small terraced houses, built and owned by the colliery owners, which typically would have two upstairs bedrooms, where the children would often sleep side by side head to foot, and a living room and kitchen downstairs. A strong desire for social distance between neighbours and a belief in the value of family privacy reinforced the norm of only family and relatives, of which there were likely to be many living locally, being allowed to visit the home on a regular basis. Friendships, as distinct from friendly relations with neighbours, did not play a large part in most adult women's lives, sandwiched as they were between the extended family network and the ever-present neighbour.

The 1920s

When boys and girls in Ferryhill left school at 14, the paths of both their social and work careers diverged sharply. Men in mining communities, whether they worked in the mines or not, were expected to work all their lives and fulfil the role of breadwinner for themselves and their families. All the male informants in this study worked as soon as they left school, and continued to work until they retired or were made redundant. Interruptions in a working life, such as short periods of unemployment, were treated as unusual and problematic occurrences which needed to be terminated as quickly as possible by the securing of alternative employment.

The relationship women had with work, by contrast, changed as their lives progressed. In the 1920s and 1930s, it was common for young girls from mining communities to enter into domestic service when they left school at 14. The economic necessity for children to contribute to the family income as soon as they could earn money was as powerful a force for daughters as it was for sons, and all the Ferryhill informants reported sending the largest part of their wages home to their parents.

Entering service had far-reaching consequences for these young women in terms of their social careers. They were taken from their homes and their families and placed among other domestic servants, sometimes from quite diverse backgrounds and different parts of the country. They also saw the lives of the privileged and wealthy at close quarters, and broadened their horizons in ways which made at least some of their brothers, who did not have the opportunity to work away from the area, envious.

For those young women who went into service, this part of their social careers represented a time when they could forge relationships with their peers independently from their families - a time of social exploration as well as hard work and limited involvement with the family. Although their work experiences varied from the pleasurable to (more commonly) the unpleasant, they all remarked how much they enjoyed being with other girls of their own age.

The length of time the informants were in domestic service varied, although the period usually lasted throughout their teenage years up until their early twenties. It is not known how common it was for domestic servants to return to their town of origin when they married, but certainly all of these informants married men from Ferryhill or nearby whom they had met during the visits home which they were able to make during their brief and infrequent holidays from domestic employment.

The 1930s

Marriage invariably meant the end of this first phase of a young woman's work career since, to quote one 72-year-old informant, 'Wives didn't work then'. Apart from work in the service industry, mainly in shops, there were very few employment opportunities for women in Ferryhill during this time and hence very few opportunities to pursue a social life outside the home. Although there were dances organised in Ferryhill during the 1930s and the first cinema (now a Bingo hall) was opened in 1936, none of the then young married women to whom I spoke half a century later remembered making use of them.

The first home for many newly-wed couples was the wife's family home, as a chronic shortage of housing often meant that the husband would move into, according to several female informants, 'my mother's house'. This arrangement could last for several years. For example, when Mrs Price married, in January 1928, her husband moved across the road from his parents' house to live in a two-bedroomed terrace house with her parents, her four brothers and three sisters for over eight years - 'not for long', she commented matter-of-factly.

The domestic demands on young wives were usually only marginally reduced by couples obtaining their own homes, as by then they had children of their own and, although they had fewer children than their parents, they had what were for the times large families, including on average five or six children to look after. Most informants agreed with Mrs Price: 'I never went out when the bairns were little - no, never.'

The 1940s

World War II had a specific social impact on life in Ferryhill in that it affected women more than it did men. For miners, life changed little, since generally they kept their jobs. They were regarded as essential workers, and were not conscripted into the armed forces; while many women contributed to the war effort by working in a local factory which was set up during the war for the filling of shell-cases.

In the spring of 1941, production started at the Royal Ordnance Factory at Aycliffe, a small town about five miles south of Ferryhill. Women were recruited from within a twenty-five-mile radius and were brought to the factory by train or bus to work one of the three daily eight- or nine-hour shifts. Ferryhill was a prime recruiting ground for the factory managers, and large numbers of local women responded to the message to contribute to the war effort.

It is with the establishment of the Ordnance Factory that a new phase begins in both the work careers and the social careers of the female informants who worked there. Although some did not like the work, complaining of the appalling conditions they had to suffer doing some of the jobs, most said they enjoyed the company of their workmates.

The 1950s

Brown (1992) comments that one of the consequences of women's employment in the filling factory was that it contributed to the changes which took place between the 1930s and the early 1950s in women's, especially married women's, participation rates. These increased employment opportunities for women were reflected in the work careers of the women informants, as only two of the women who worked in the filling factory returned to the home after the war and did not work again. The rest found work, if not in Ferryhill, then in the nearby towns of Newton Aycliffe and Spennymoor where factories were established in the new trading estates .

Alongside this development in women's work careers came parallel developments in their social careers. Two consequences of these developments stand out: the women informants talked about friends in a way that hitherto in their life stories they had not and, in the more formal and public social realm, there was evidence of the rise of the voluntary club, which in Ferryhill was predominantly the domain of women.

The 1960s and after

The life stories of all the women are characterised by a concentration on activities inside the home and a corresponding lack of participation, at least for the first forty or fifty years of their lives, in leisure institutions in the town on anything like the scale of the local men's. Nearly all of the seventeen women (out of the sixty-one female informants of the screening survey) who said they went to the Workingmen's Club attended the 'Ladies' Night' at one of the Clubs held once a fortnight, but three of them were married and were accompanied by their husbands.

The older women of Ferryhill responded to their near exclusion from organised social life in the town not by breaking down this traditional division between the sexes but by extending and entrenching it. No attempt was being made to change the nature of the existing local leisure institutions, which were fashioned out of male social needs and which therefore catered principally for men. Rather, new institutions were formed whose activities were populated almost exclusively by women, who for the first time could legitimately congregate independently of their men in a public place, away from the home and the street.

Bulmer (1978) was the first to identify this trend, noting that, by the mid 1970s, there were many voluntary organisations in the mining villages in County Durham which were mainly the preserve of women, and adding, 'indeed, the division between the sexes [in this respect] is striking' (p.32). In 1982, when the fieldwork for this study took place, there were several voluntary organisations and commercial ventures in Ferryhill dominated by women both in their organisational structure and in their clientele. Some, such as the Tea Dance and Pop-In, organised by Age Concern, and the Over Sixties club, were specifically geared to older people, while others were offshoots of religious organisations, an example being the Catholic Women's League. There were also secular organisations such as the Women's Institute, which did not advertise itself as being specifically for older people but which nevertheless tended to attract women beyond, or approaching, the age of retirement. Lastly, there were commercially-run activities that catered for women, the most popular being the

Bingo sessions held every weekday evening in the building that used to house the cinema.

A significant minority of older women in Ferryhill had fashioned their social lives around the activities of these organisations. Significantly if unsurprisingly, very few men attended these activities. There was ample evidence from the women who did attend these activities that they were popular and important social events. As well as cementing neighbourly relationships and extending some into friendships, participation had, for some informants, made possible the resurrection of old friendships and acquaintanceships after long periods of separation.

The social origins of the Old People's Clubs in Ferryhill should be understood as much in terms of the particular cultural processes evident in mining communities as of the more general socio-economic forces of an increasingly affluent society or of a growth in the proportion of elderly people in the population. The rise of female-orientated leisure institutions in Ferryhill can be traced, via the life stories, to the period just after the Second World War. Before that time, women stayed in the home, and only left the neighbourhood to attend church or chapel or to go to dances or, from the 1930s on, the cinema. Participation by women in paid employment during the war and in subsequent years helped create openings for women in their social careers.

This is not to suggest that there was a direct, causal relationship between increased participation in work and increased participation in leisure activities. Rather, the social benefits of work in enabling women to associate independently with their peers helped to create a sociable atmosphere among women conducive to their taking advantage of the new opportunities for socialising brought about by the comparative affluence of the years following the Second World War.

Conclusion

The evolution of the social lives of women in Ferryhill over the course of this century was traced by situating their life stories within their historical and cultural context. There are dangers inherent in this method: in particular, the aggregating of life stories into time sequences, in this instance into decades, can obscure the uniqueness of each person's life story and give the false impression that social life in Ferryhill allowed no room for individual response and action. The socio-cultural framework exposed by this approach, that of a life course for women characterised by changing employment possibilities and social opportunities, was constructed by looking for the similarities in the life stories. It must be acknowledged, however, that at each stage there were informants who did not conform to the more general story that was unfolding. Space does not allow for a broader and more subtle narrative to be developed in this chapter. Nevertheless, the life story method does allow us to tap older people's memories and so develop an analysis that views the present from a historical perspective.

References

Abrams, P. (1982) *Historical Sociology*. Shepton Mallett, Somerset: Open Books.

Austrin, T. and Beynon, H. (1981) *Global Outpost: Working Class Experience of Big Business in the NE of England 1964-1979*. Durham: University of Durham Mimeograph.

Bertaux, D. (ed.) (1981) *Biography and Society: The Life History Approach in the Social Sciences*. London: Sage.

Bertaux, D. and Kohli, M. (1984) 'The life story approach: a continental view', *Annual Review of Sociology*, 10, pp.215-37.

Beynon, H., Hudson, R. and Sadler, D. (1991) *A Tale of Two Industries: The Contraction of Coal and Steel in the North East of England*. Buckingham: Open University Press.

Brown, R. (1992) 'World war, women's work and the gender division of paid labour' in S. Arber and N. Gilbert (eds.) *Women and Working Lives: Divisions and Change*. London: Macmillan.

Bulmer, M. (1978) 'Social structure and social change in the twentieth-century' in M. Bulmer (ed.) *Mining and Social Change: Durham County in the Twentieth Century*. London: Croom Helm.

Dennis, N., Henriques, F. and Slaughter ,C. (1976) *Coal Is Our Life: An Analysis of a Yorkshire Mining Community*. London: Tavistock.

Gearing, B. and Dant, T. (1990) 'Doing biographical research' in S. M. Peace (ed.) *Researching Social Gerontology: Concepts, Methods and Issues*. London: Sage.

House, J.W. and Knight, E.M. (1967) *Pit Closure and the*

Community. Papers on Migration and Mobility in Northern England No. 5. Newcastle: Department of Geography, University of Newcastle upon Tyne.

Humphrey, R. (1993a) 'Life stories and social careers: ageing and social life in an ex-mining town', *Sociology*, 27(1), pp.166-78.

Humphrey, R. (1993b) 'The life story method as historical ethnography', Paper Presented at the Annual Conference of the British Sociological Association, University of Kent.

Humphrey, R. (1993c) *Social Participation and Life Stories of Elderly People in an Ex-Mining Town*. Unpublished PhD Thesis, University of Newcastle upon Tyne.

Lockwood, D. (1966) 'Sources of variation in working-class images of society', *The Sociological Review*, 14: 249-67.

Lummis, T. (1987) *Listening to History: The Authenticity of Oral Evidence*. London: Hutchinson.

Plummer, K. (1990) *Documents of Life: An Introduction to the Problems and Literature of a Humanistic Method*. Reissue. London: Unwin Hyman.

Qureshi, H. and Walker, A. (1989) *The Caring Relationship: Elderly People and Their Families*. London: Macmillan.

Roberts, R. (1971) *The Classic Slum: Salford Life in the First Quarter of the Century*. Manchester: Manchester University Press.

Ross, E. (1983) 'Survival networks: women's neighbourhood sharing in London before World War I', *History Workshop Journal*, 15, pp.4-27.

Strauss, A. and Corbin, J. (1990) *Basics of Qualitative Research: Grounded Theory Procedures and Techniques*. London: Sage.

Taylor, R.C. (1966) *The Implications of Migration from the Durham Coalfield*. Unpublished PhD Thesis, University of Durham.

Toennies, F. (1957) *Community and Society (Gemeinschaft und Gesellschaft)* (translated and edited by C.P. Loomis). East Lansing, Mich.: Michigan State University Press.

Wenger, G.C. (1984) *The Supportive Network: Coping with Old Age*. London: Allen & Unwin.

Young, M. and Wilmott, P. (1957) *Family and Kinship in East London*. Harmondsworth: Penguin.

A solemn joyousness: death and dying in Tibetan Buddhism

BRIAN HOLTON

> Worn out garments are shed by the body;
> Worn out bodies are shed by the dweller.
> *Bhagavad Gita*

Death is not final. Nor is it a single event. Each death is a link in the chain of sorrows which binds us to the cycle of death and rebirth, and it is our own actions, thoughts and intentions which forge that chain.

That is the message of Buddhism, beginning with the Four Noble Truths expounded by the Buddha in his first post-enlightenment teaching:

> Life is painful: all sentient beings suffer
>   birth, sickness and death.
> Pain is caused by craving for existence.
> To end that craving is to end suffering.
> There is a way to end suffering:
>   the Eightfold Path of the Buddha.

Not to recognise these truths is ignorance, and it is ignorance which lengthens our chain of sorrows. It is a failure to recognise the distinction between real and unreal, between transient and eternal and, because it prevents us from taking the path which will release us from suffering, it enmeshes us in delusion. The Eightfold Path consists of a series of necessary conditions or states to be achieved where we become masters over our own minds by constant attention to right thought, resolve, speech, conduct, livelihood, effort, mindfulness and concentration (i.e. meditation practice). By constant discipline we can free ourselves from the craving to exist (or not to exist), and so break the chain of suffering and wake to the liberation of enlightenment, to the free mind.

Death is no cause for grief, since it is an opportunity to wake to the supreme reality, perhaps the best such opportunity we may have in a lifetime.

The *Bardo Thödol* or *Tibetan Book of the Dead* (trans. Evans-Wentz, 1957 and Freemantle and Chögyam Trungpa, 1975) is a teaching text from the 14th century which relies on an oral tradition reaching back to the 8th century and to the great Kashmiri missionary to Tibet, Padmasambhava (also called Guru Rinpoche or 'precious guru'). It contains the text of a ritual intended to be read to a dying person, explaining what is happening during the process of dying and in the post-mortem state, when consciousness continues. Its aim is to ease the dead person's passage through a three-stage process where each stage offers the deceased the chance of liberation through recognition of the true nature of mind. It is also used to guide meditation, and as a wisdom text containing teachings which are necessary to right living. Chögyam Trungpa (1973) writes of it:

> ...this book is not only a message for those who are going to die and for those who are already dead, but it is also a message for those who are already born; birth and death apply to everybody constantly, at this very moment.

To understand this, we must first realise that in Buddhism the self is held to be a delusion created by the fundamental intellectual error of presupposing a division between the 'I' and the 'not-I', between the subject and the object. We believe, in other words, that we are discrete selves dissociated from the world; the result of this is an attachment to and a dependence on an ego which, by its craving for existence, gives birth to alienation, desire and enmity and so fuels the endless cycle of birth and death. (That is the meaning of the third Noble Truth: to end the delusion of separateness is to end the self's craving to be, and so to end suffering.)

Secondly, a further product of this error is the delusion of continuity, or the failure to recognise transience. *All* phenomena are transient:

> Thus shall you think of all this fleeting
>   world:
> A star at dawn, a bubble in a stream,

A flash of lightning in a summer cloud.
A phantom, an illusion, a dream.
Diamond Sutra

No form is more substantial than the patterns of sunlight on water. Forms arise out of ultimate reality just as fleeting thoughts gather, take shape, and disperse. 'In the highest sense', says the Pali work *The Path of Purity,* 'beings have only a very short instant to live, only so long as a moment of consciousness lasts'. We are, in this highest sense, being born and dying at every moment in a process which, in contrast to corporeal death (the cessation of physical functions), is called 'continuous death'.

Life and death, then, are two different aspects of the single unbroken flow of reality: only our ignorance divides them. Grof and Halifax observe:

Death and life, usually considered to be irreconcilable opposites, appear to be dialectically interrelated. Living fully and with maximum awareness every moment of one's life leads to an accepting and reconciled attitude toward death (cited in de Spelder and Strickland, 1983, p.405).

This is an apt description of the Buddhist view.

The *Book of the Dead*'s Tibetan title means 'liberation through hearing' (*thödol*) 'in an intermediate state' (*bardo*). *Bardo* in origin means a gap, or a break in continuity. There are six bardos identified: those of birth, dreaming and meditation occur as 'suspended states' in life; those of the moment of death, supreme reality and becoming (to which the book's title refers) occur in the post-mortem state. A bardo in this sense is an instant in which our delusion of separateness is suspended and it is possible, if we are alert enough and our mind is disciplined, to recognise ultimate reality. The Buddhist practitioner's discipline is a preparation for such a gap, such an instant when the light of reality floods in.

The process of dying, as understood in the Tibetan Buddhist tradition and set out in *Bardo Thödol*, begins with the gradual decay of the aggregates whose incessant interaction give rise to the delusion of ego - the five *skhandas* of corporeality, sensation, perception, mental formation and consciousness. As each in the sequence decays, so external reality falls away, and the moment of death arrives. (In the west, death is defined as occurring after only the first of these five aggregates has decayed: dying is thus a lengthier process than we had imagined.) The bardo of this moment is experienced as an intensely bright light. This luminosity is explained as the neutral ground of ultimate reality, the seamless garment of 'Buddha-nature', which is the immutable and eternal nature of all beings and the true nature of mind:

> The nature of everything is open, empty
> and naked like the sky.
> Luminous emptiness, without centre
> or circumference...
>
> *Bardo Thödol*

Our receptivity to that light is conditioned by our previous actions. The operation of the law of causes and effects (karma) ensures that what we are now is a direct result of what we have been in the past. If our past actions, thoughts, desires and so on have meant that we have not accumulated pure karma (i.e. that we have failed to free ourselves from delusions or from persistent ignorance), then our impure karma will obscure that light. Pure karma, on the other hand, will allow us to recognise that reality, and to enter into another mode of existence by snuffing out all trace of our separated self in the moment of nirvana (that is, the merging of the individual, transient self into the ultimate reality of Buddha-nature). To do so is to escape the chain of sorrows, to step off the wheel of birth and death: it is to be liberated.

Failing liberation, the newly-dead person falls into a state of unconsciousness lasting three or four days, during which time a 'body of consciousness' is formed: it is this consciousness which perceives all that follows in the post-mortem state.

The second bardo, the bardo of supreme reality, finds the consciousness waking to luminosity again, to perceive over the next 14 days the manifestation of 42 peaceful and 58 wrathful 'deities'. These are also known as 'forms of manifestation', and are symbols of the energies necessary to or helpful for liberation. The function of the wrathful ones is to attack ignorance or illusions which hinder spiritual growth and development. A further chance to realise the nature of mind is presented here, but if the consciousness fails to recognise these 'deities' as projections of his or her own self which have been triggered by his or her own karmic reflexes, then the third bardo dawns.

The bardo of becoming dawns with the realisation that the person no longer has a body, and is driven by the craving to possess a body again. The initial stages, which may last from one to three weeks, are spent reliving the actions of the life just ended, in preparation for the final week of searching for rebirth. We choose our birth: the consciousness finds itself drawn to a particular realm - the human world, the world of the gods, or a variety of hells - in a manner wholly determined by the individual's karma. As we have acted, so we condition what we will be. the American Zen teacher Philip Kapleau notes:

> Rebirth arises from two causes: the last thought of the previous life as the governing principle and the actions of the previous life as its basis. The stopping of the last thought is known as decease; the appearance of the first thought as rebirth. Visions of copulating couples draw the consciousness out of the post-mortem state and into rebirth. So the cycle begins again (cited in de Spelder and Strickland, 1983, p.469, in footnote).

The key concept behind the 49-day post-mortem process is that every sentient being *is* Buddha-nature. To realise this, to wake up to the delusion of the separate self, is to become aware of the vastness of our own nature. Death is then 'the culmination of a lifetime's spiritual practice' (Sögyal Rinpoche, 1992). By alerting us to what happens at death and beyond, *Bardo Thödol* acts as an itinerary and guides us in our preparation for the inevitable moment of dying.

Now, this is all very interesting, but why do we need to know about it? I would suggest that, apart from the obvious anthropological, sociological or philosophical interest, an engagement with the ideas of the *Bardo Thödol* may help us redefine our own ideas on death and dying, which in turn may help us to improve our methods of coping with bereavement, with counselling and assisting the dying, and with dealing with our own exit from this life.

The function of the *Bardo Thödol* and its associated ritual is to provide a conceptual framework and a set of practices for dealing with death. For the dying, the bereaved and the practitioner alike it gives a clear and detailed explanation of the nature of mind, to which ritual adds the meaningful structure it imports to the chaos of lived experience. Can we in the west feel confident that we can effectively do the same?

It may of course be said that the *Bardo Thödol* is a unique product of a unique culture, and that, while knowledge of it may be helpful in dealing with natives of that culture, it is too exotic to be of any use to us. Leaving aside the question of the growing number of western Buddhists, such an ethnocentric view would have to be set against a body of evidence from our own culture. For instance, Grof and Halifax found in the course of their work with psychedelics such as LSD that:

> ...subjects unsophisticated in anthropology and mythology experience images, episodes, and even entire thematic sequences that bear a striking resemblance to the descriptions of the posthumous journey of the soul and the death-rebirth mysteries of various cultures

and concluded that:

> ...the human unconscious contains matrices for a wide variety of experiences that constitute the basic elements of the spiritual journey of the dying (cited in de Spelder and Strickland, 1983, p.405)..

For over a thousand years Tibetan Buddhism has been developing and refining a consistent body of knowledge about death and dying. Tibetan death ritual stresses not grief but joy, not the community's or the family's loss, but the deceased's opportunity to achieve liberation. The *Bardo Thödol* deserves our attention because its aim is to help us die, not in fear and ignorance, but with clarity of purpose and, in Tucci's (1980) memorable phrase, with a 'solemn joyousness'.

References and Further Reading

Chögyam Trungpa (1973) *Cutting Through Spiritual Materialism*. Berkeley, California: Shambhala.

de Spelder, L.A. and Strickland, A.C. (1983) *The Last Dance: Encountering Death and Dying*. Palo Alto, California: Mayfield.

Evans-Wentz, W.E. (1957) *The Tibetan Book of the Dead*. Oxford: OUP.

Freemantle, F. and Chögyam Trungpa (1975) *The Tibetan Book of the Dead*. London: Rider.

Govinda, Lama Anagarika (1959) *Foundations of Tibetan Mysticism*. London: Rider.

Sögyal Rinpoche (1992) *The Tibetan Book of Living and Dying*. London: Rider.

Tarthang Tulku (1977) *Gesture of Balance*. Berkeley, California.

Tucci, G. (1980) *The Religions of Tibet*. London.

Speculating about the future

PETER KAIM-CAUDLE

Projecting Size and Age Composition

In speculating about the future of an ageing population some 30 or 40 years ahead, estimating the number of older people and their age and sex composition is one of the easier tasks. The United Kingdom (UK) population aged 60 years or older in 2020 will consist of those aged 30 years or older in 1990 less those who die or emigrate during these 30 years plus the immigrants who, after taking account of mortality, will be 60 years or older in 2020. Estimated age specific mortality, based on a study of trends and stated assumptions, has in the past declined in a fairly predictable manner. Fluctuations in migration of the relevant age groups have been too small to have had a marked effect on the population aged 60 years and older. It seems reasonable to assume that this will be the same in future. The population projections of this age group by the Office of Population Censuses and Surveys (OPCS) have therefore been fairly accurate (see Table 1).

An evaluation of the economic and social impact of changes in the number of the older population makes it necessary also to know the future size of other age groups. Total population projections include estimates of the number of births, which in recent decades have fluctuated widely, and this has led to widely differing estimates of future births and of the size of future populations. For example the projections of birth for 1990 made in 1965 were about twice those made in 1955 and the projections of the total population for 1990 made in 1965 were about a quarter higher than those made in 1955 (see Table 1). This explains why the future proportion of the total population who will be 60 years or older is more difficult to forecast than their number. The population projections of the OPCS are now based on more sophisticated techniques than

Speculating about the future

Table 1
Projected UK demographic data in 1955 and 1965 for 1990

	Recorded in 1990	Projection for 1990 in	
		1955	1965
Total population (millions)	57.4	53.1	66.8
Population over 60 yrs (millions)	11.9	11.4	11.5
Number of births (000s)	799	660	1300

Sources
1. *For 1990, Office of Population Censuses and Surveys (1991), p. 59 and p.62.*
2. *Birth projections in 1955 and 1965, Central Policy Review Staff (1977).*
3. *Total population and population over 60 years, projections in 1955 and 1965: Central Statistical Office (1956) p.11 and (1966) p.13.*

those employed in the 1950s and 1960s, but all the same estimates of the future size of the older population will always be more reliable than those of their proportion of the total population.

Traditionally, and in United Nations publications, the old age dependency ratio is defined as the number of people aged 65 years or more as a proportion of the population aged 15 to 64 years. This is meant to express the burden on the population of working age of supporting the population past working age. However, in the UK in the circumstances of the 1990s, both the lower and the upper limit of working age seem inappropriate. The minimum school leaving age is now 16 years, an increasing proportion of young people aged 16 to 19 years are still in full-time education and more than ever are attending college up to their early or even middle twenties. The normal retirement age for men is still 65 years (it has been 60 years for women since 1940) but only a minority of men retire that late. In 1990 only 49 per cent of men age 60-64 years were still working. The remainder received occupational pensions, unemployment compensation of various types, invalidity pensions or unearned income such as interest on capital, dividends or rents, while others were supporting themselves out of their savings or redundancy pay. It is therefore more appropriate in present conditions to define the old age dependency ratio as the number

Table 2

Projected changes in demographic data between 1990 and 2020 in the UK and the Federal Republic of Germany[1]

	UK			FRG[1]		
Population age	1990	2020	Change %	1990	2020	Change %
0-19 yrs (millions)	14.9	14.9	-	13.1	10.3	- 21
20-59 yrs (millions)	30.5	31.4	+ 3	36.5	31.0	- 13
60 plus yrs (millions)	11.9	14.4	+21	13.1	17.5	+34
Total (millions)	57.3	60.7	+ 6	62.7	58.8	- 6
80 plus yrs (millions)	2.1	2.7	+29	2.4	3.7	+54
Pop'n 20-59 yrs per 100 aged 60 yrs plus (n)	256	218	- 15	278	177	- 36
Half pay pensions[2] Levy on gross pay (%)	16.3	18.7	+14	15.4	22.0	+43

1   *As constituted prior to 1991.*
2   *See text and Appendix.*
Source: Eurostat (1991) Table B-13 and 1-12

of people aged 60 years and older as a proportion of the population aged 20 to 59 years.

The OPCS projects an increase in the UK population aged 60 years and older from 11.9 million in 1990 to 14.4 million in 2020. This is an increase of 21 per cent over 30 years, or an average annual increase of about 0.7 per cent. During this period the population below and of working age is projected to increase only marginally. The total population projections for 2020 are based on estimates of the number of births over the 30 years period 1990 to 2020 while the projections of the working population are based on estimates of the number of births for only the ten year period from 1990 to 2000 and are therefore more reliable (see Table 2).

In passing it is of interest to note that during these thirty years the population of Germany (FRG) is projected to age much more rapidly than that of the UK. The population of working age is projected to decline by 13 per cent and that below working age by 21 per cent while that above the age of 60 years is projected to increase by 34 per cent and that above 80 years by 54 per cent. While in 1990 there were 278 people of working age for every 100 past working age this number by 2020 is projected to decline to 177 (see Table 2).

Retirement Pensions

The projected population changes in the UK would result in a decline of the number of people of working age per 100 people past working age from 256 in 1990 to 218 in 2020. The burden on the population of working age of supporting the population past working age on 'half pay' (half of their average gross earnings less the required pension levy) would increase from 16.3 per cent to 18.7 per cent of gross earnings (for calculation see Appendix). This increase of 2.4 per cent of gross earnings is about the same percentage increase over thirty years as the average annual increase in GNP during the last 40 years.

An annual increase of 2.4 per cent over the next 30 years would increase real earnings, in line with GNP, by about 100 per cent. So that in 1990 for every £100 of gross earnings net earnings, after deducting the pension levy of 16.3 per cent, would have been £83.7 while in 2020 for every £200 of gross earnings net earnings, after the deduction of the pension levy of 18.7 per cent, would be £162.6. If the age distribution in 2020 had remained the same as it was in 1990 (256 persons aged 20-59 years for every 100 aged 60 years or more) net earnings in 2020 would have been £167.4 that means £4.8, or about three per cent, higher than on the projected less favourable age distribution, in 2020. The projected changes would also reduce the half pay pension by £2.4. On the quite reasonable assumption made, the unfavourable changes in the age composition would reduce net earnings of the population of working age only to quite a minimal extent.

Since 1979 the social insurance retirement pension provisions have been reduced twice. Prior to 1980 pensions were adjusted annually in line with changes in prices or average earnings whichever was the greater. Thereafter the adjustment was only in line with prices. In 1986, the benefit formula of the State Earnings Related Pension Scheme (SERPS) was altered so as to reduce future pension payments. At the same time incentives were provided to encourage occupational and personal pension schemes. Personal pension schemes relate pensions not to pre-retirement earnings but to the value, at the time of retirement, of the premiums invested during working life. Occupational 'contribution fixed' schemes which are increasingly replacing 'benefit fixed' schemes have the same characteristics. Both provide at best partial and often no adjustment for post-retirement changes in prices or earnings.

The reduction in social insurance pensions and the encouragement of private and occupational pensions were mainly motivated by political considerations. As is demonstrated above, they were not required by the projected demographic changes.

In assessing the burden of supporting the population past working age their ratio to the number of people of working age is only one of four relevant factors. The other three are the level of pensions, the proportion of the population of working age who will be in remunerative employment and the productivity (value of output per man/woman year) of that population. The level of pensions is a political decision which will be influenced by many considerations some of which pull in opposite directions. Two of the most important will be the rate of growth of the GNP and the proportion of pensioners in the population. A high proportion will result in high aggregate costs of pensions and this will encourage low levels of pensions, but a high proportion will also strengthen the voting power of pensioners and this will encourage high levels of pensions. Any prediction of pension level thirty years ahead can thus be no more than a guess. The same applies to the rate of labour force participation. Since the 1970s this has declined for men and increased for women. Its level thirty years ahead will depend on innumerable, partly contradictory factors which can not be predicted with any confidence. While an increase in productivity, largely due to advances in technology, to capital investment and to a more educated labour force, seems fairly certain, any prediction of the rate of increase must be subject to wide margins of error. Over a thirty year period a rate of increase of 2 and a half per cent will double the GNP, a rate of 4 and three quarters per cent will quadruple it.

If fertility in the UK remains at its 1990 level (that means about one eighth below replacement level) the burden of an ageing population will be more severe in the 30 years between 2020 and 2050 than it is likely to be in the preceding thirty years. None of the population of working age in 2050 will have been born in 1990. As has been shown above the estimates of future births are subject to wide margins of error. It is possible to estimate, on stated assumptions, the size of population groups for many decades ahead, but the longer the period for which projections are made the greater is the probability that the projection will be erroneous.

Most earnings related occupations, social security and public service pension schemes have the characteristic that the level of pensions of younger pensioners is higher than that of older pensioners. This is most markedly the case for recipients of pensions which are not or only, partially, adjusted for price changes. Between the first quarter of 1983 and the last quarter of 1992 the UK Retail Price Index (RPI) increased by 68 per cent (Bissett, 1993, p.3), so that annuities and non index-linked pensions during these years lost 40 per cent of their purchasing power. Index-linked earnings related pensions maintain their purchasing power, but pay lower pensions for older than for younger pensioners. For example - pensioners who retired on half pay in 1992, when average real (adjusted for price changes) earnings were 25 per cent higher than they had been in 1983 (Bissett, 1993, p.3), will receive higher pensions than pensioners who retired on half pay in 1983. Public service pensions for teachers, civil servants, doctors and nurses, the State Earnings Related Pension Scheme (SERPS) and the German social insurance scheme provide, on the assumption of rising real wages, for each generation of pensioners higher pensions than were received by the preceding generation. In some schemes, particularly in earnings related compulsory social insurance schemes, the number of pensioners over 75 years will increase faster than that of younger pensioners. As older pensioners receive lower pensions than younger pensioners the cost of pensions will therefore increase less than the number of pensioners.

The British contributory basic flat rate retirement pension is the same for all pensioners irrespective of age with the minor exception of an increase of a paltry 25p per week for pensioners over 80 years. This pension is index-linked, but not related to changes in earnings so that pensioners do not participate in the rising standard of living of the population of working age. The widening gap between pension and wage levels can be reduced by ad hoc increases in the basic retirement pension.

Health and Community Services

The average cost of health and community services increases with age, especially after the age of 70 years. The ageing of the population and the resulting changes in the age composition will therefore increase the cost of these services, other things remaining the same, by considerably more than the small projected increase in the population. If it is assumed that the average cost for the population past the retirement age of 60 years was in 1990 about three times and will in 2021 (due to the ageing of the retired population) be about four times that of the population of working age, the cost of these services for the adult population (over 20 years) will increase by approximately a third, an average increase of the magnitude of one per cent per year.

It is not likely that everything except demographic data will remain the same. Greater understanding of the causes of illness, more sophisticated procedures, more effective medicines and more expensive equipment may increase or decrease the cost of a spell of illness or even prevent some illnesses. An increase in the standard of these services irrespective of their effectiveness would also result in higher costs. Such increased standards in health services might include less or even no delay for consultant appointments and for hospital admissions, as is the case in France and the FRG, and more single and double bedded wards. In community care, increased standards might include more liberal criteria for admission to nursing and old people's homes, less severe means tests, higher staffing ratios in these homes and more domestic help and community nursing for elderly people.

The factors which influence the cost and economic benefits of rehabilitating, curing, treating and caring for old people who are ill, frail or handicapped are complex. For elderly people, the benefit will rarely take the form of enabling them to contribute to the GNP by taking up remunerative employment. Successful treatment may however not only improve their quality of life and that of their families, but reduce the older person's need for support. Thus a successful operation on an elderly woman for the removal of a cataract, or the replacement of a hip joint will restore her ability to look after herself. This may result in several economic benefits. It may free the daughter who looked after her for remunerative employment or it may enable the older woman to dispense with all or some of the community services which she received. All the same it seems probable that the economic, in contrast to the social, benefits of providing health and community services for older people are relatively small.

Costs are somewhat easier to measure than benefits. For a proper assessment of cost, all costs incurred irrespective of who incurs them must be considered. For example a reduction in the length of average hospital stays will reduce the cost of hospitalisation but may increase the cost of GP and community services. The increased cost of these services may take different forms. There may be higher remuneration for GPs, other members of the primary health care team and other community service staff to compensate them for their increased workload. Alternatively there may be an increase in the number of staff employed in these services. Lastly (and this is the most probable outcome) the hours worked by GPs and all other staff will remain the same. The hours spent in looking after early discharged hospital patients will be offset by spending less time on other patients and clients. These others, most of whom will be elderly, will bear the 'cost' of the early discharges by receiving lower level of services. Early hospital discharge may also result in greater burdens on the families of discharged patients. A cost which can not easily be quantified. Another example of a transfer of cost are more expensive medications. If these result in the avoidance or shortening of hospitalisation they may well reduce the aggregate cost of health services, despite the increase in the drug bill.

The widely held view that an increase in the effectiveness and efficiency of health services would tend to reduce their cost is of dubious validity. As efficiency is defined as the input of resources per unit of output it seems to follow that an increase in efficiency must reduce cost. In practice due to the unlimited demand for health services, for which no charge is made, and due to friction - immobility, long training, indivisibility and political considerations - in the medical labour market this is often not the case. If increased efficiency reduces the time of a particular operation from four to two hours, surgeons and their supporting staff will now be able to perform twice the number of this operation or increase the number of other operations in this speciality or be retrained for other surgical work. In all three contingencies there will be an increased cost of hotel and nursing services and therefore of aggregate NHS cost. Only if the surgeon and their supporting staff are made redundant, a not very likely contingency, will aggregate NHS cost decline. In the long run, in which most of us are dead, increased efficiency will tend to reduce aggregate costs but this is often not the case in the immediate future. Fixed hospital budgets will restrain the trend towards increased cost of changes in supply, for example increased efficiency, or in demand, for example the ageing of the population.

Hip joint replacement and removal of cataract are good examples of improved effectiveness. If they were not possible the quality of life of many older people would be much worse, but NHS cost would be less. However the cost to community services of caring for blind and immobile people would be higher.

Increases in the effectiveness of health services which prolong life may be socially desirable, but tend to increase cost for two quite distinct reasons. First they frequently use expensive equipment and employ expensive procedures. Second, and more important, the patient who would have died would not have needed any health services in future while the surviving patient will require more health services in future. It is already possible to prolong the life of patients who suffer a very low quality of life, often at very great expense. In future the ability to sustain life may well increase more rapidly than the ability to maintain or restore a reasonable quality of life (whatever this may mean). In such circumstances the validity of the dictum 'Thou shalt not kill, but need not strive officiously to keep alive' will be widely debated. Ageism, discrimination on account of old age, is as undesirable in access to health services as it is in other spheres of life. In rich countries like the UK, in which the annual average increase of the GNP per head is above two and a half per cent, the resources ought to be available for everybody irrespective of age to receive all effective health services which substantially improve their quality of life. This may require a reconsideration of medical ethics and public policy which tends to consider the preservation of life more important, deserving more resources, than improving the quality of life (Andrews, 1993; Gillon, 1993).

In recent years it has been public policy to reduce the

numbers of beds in geriatric wards, long stay mental hospitals and Social Services Department (SSD) old people's homes. The former patients, clients and other frail elderly people are to receive residential and domiciliary community services. The residential services are to be provided largely by private companies and monitored by SSDs while domiciliary services, at least for the present, are being provided mainly by NHS Trust and SSDs. There are considerable differences of opinion about the extent to which private enterprise is able to provide reasonable standards of services at reasonable cost to these very vulnerable people. They lack almost all the characteristics which are required for the successful working of market forces.

No charges are made for long term NHS beds while for residential community care the clients and patients have to pay the charges which the providers make, subject to a means and income test (Kellett, 1993). The switch to community care will thus reduce public expenditure. The recipient of community care will have to apply all their income, except a small pocket money allowance and all their capital, except £8,000, to pay for residential community services. For people who have no income except their pensions and only a little capital this switch will make no difference, but for people who have other income, are house owners or possess capital the new arrangements will be a great burden - possibly £12,000 to £25,000 per year. It is more than likely that there will be considerable evasion and avoidance of these charges.

As only a comparatively small proportion of elderly people require residential care and as the incidence of this need varies widely among individuals, the provision of such care as a social insurance benefit would be quite feasible. Such a compulsory social insurance scheme has just been introduced in Germany.

Ageism

Ageism, the disadvantaging of the older people for irrelevant reasons, like racism, sexism and other types of discrimination is often the product of two fallacies. The first is the erroneous attribution of undesirable characteristics to a particular category of people. The second is the illogical claim that all people in that category have an undesirable characteristic because some people in that category have or are alleged to have this characteristic. However people who avowedly discriminate may claim with varying degrees of justification that their conduct is validated by experience and probability and involves less time and expense than fair and reasonable conduct. Another important factor which makes for discrimination is that it serves the economic and social interest of those who benefit from discrimination. Certain categories of people may be disadvantaged in employment, housing, access to education, health care and social facilities. In addition to material and visible disadvantages people who are discriminated against often feel demeaned and are considered demeaned by others. This is certainly true of older people.

Some disadvantaging of older people occurs in all spheres of life, but it is most important in employment and to a lesser and more debatable extent in access to health services. In employment, people above a certain age are often disadvantaged in recruitment, training, promotion and redundancy. This is usually the result of the two fallacies to which reference has been made but may also be due to some arbitrary rules. People may not be recruited because they are too old to pay sufficient contributions to retire on an adequate pension, or because a particular age composition of the labour force is required to implement an organisation's promotion policy.

Negative and erroneous concepts about older people are wide spread. Old age is often associated with lack of enterprise, slowness, unreliability, ill health and poverty. There is little appreciation of the wide diversity in the rate of ageing and the differences in the state of health and fitness of older people of the same age.

Peter Forster (1993), in a recent paper reviews the relationship between health and age. His three major conclusions are:

> There is no evidence to support the common assumption that older workers are slower and less productive.
>
> While some slowing down undoubtedly occurs with age, the effects are greatly exaggerated and can usually be offset by changing the pattern or intensity of the work.
>
> Research overwhelmingly supports the proposition that age is a poor predictor of performance and ability.

The Sex Discrimination Acts 1975 and 1986 and the Race Relations Act 1976 have been successful in reducing, but not eliminating sexism and racism in employment. The implementation of equal pay for equal work has involved an increase in cost of many billions of pounds (in current values). Women's wages in many occupations were raised to those of men and this led to increases in prices and taxes. Legislation against racism however involved virtually no economic cost and the same would be the case for anti ageist legislation. There might however be some redistribution of income in favour of the over-50s and there is a strong probability that output would increase.

An Age Discrimination Act might include a prohibition of any upper age limit in recruitment advertising, the elimination of mandatory retirement and changes in pension law. The government supports the abolition of ageist policies, aims to promote good employment practices and encourages the most effective use of human resources. It endeavours however to obtain these objectives by exhortation rather than legislation. The ideology of the present government is against legislation as it wants to minimise interference with the discretion of employers, wants 'to get the state off people's backs' and believes that citizens know better than the state what benefits them. The USA has had an Age Discrimination Act since 1967. This prohibits arbitrary age discrimination in employment and makes it unlawful 'to limit, segregate or classify an employee in any way that would deprive that employee of job opportunities or adversely affect employment status because of their age' (quoted from Forster, 1993). In 1978 the earliest mandatory retirement age was fixed at 70 years.

Conclusion

To sum up, over the next 30 years the circumstances of life of older people in the UK in respect of pensions, health and community services and age discrimination will be mainly determined by government policy and possibly increasingly by that of the European Community. The impact of the ageing of the population will be much less important, especially in comparison with many other European countries, notably Germany, where the population will age more rapidly.

Appendix: Calculating Pension Levies

The burden on the population of working age of paying pensions to the population past working age can be illustrated by an example based on three assumptions. First, persons aged 20 to 59 years, including those who have no earned income, earn on average £100 per week. Second, all persons aged 60 years or older receive a pension equivalent to one half of the net earnings (gross earnings less pension levy) of the population of working age. Third, the pensions of the population past working age are financed by pension levies on the population of working age. In 1990 there were 256 people of working age for every 100 people past working age. On the above assumptions, the aggregate income of 256 people of working age was (256 x £100) £25,600 which had to be shared between 256 people of working age and 100 past working age. As the later are to receive half pay - half of the net earnings of those of working age, their aggregate pension would be the same as the net earnings of 50 people of working age. The average net earnings of people of working age would thus be (£25,600÷306) = £83.66 and pensions would be (£83.66÷2) = £41.83. The average pension levy would be (£100 - £83.66) = £16.34. The aggregate pension levy would be (256 x £16.34) = £4,183, the same as the aggregate pensions paid (100 x £41.83) = £4,183. In 2020 when the projected number of people of working age per 100 people past working age will be 218, the pension levy required to provide half pay pensions will be £18.66, an increase of £2.32 (£18.66 - £16.34) over a 30 year period. As gross earnings of £100 per week are assumed the pension levy in 1990 and 2020 would be 16.3 per cent and 18.7 per cent respectively, an increase of 2.4 per cent of gross earnings.

The above example is meant to illustrate on certain assumptions the cost of financing increased pension payments to the projected increase in the number of people past working age in 2020. The costs are related to earnings, a large component of the GNP. The assumptions made, while not unreasonable, are quite arbitrary. The assumed working age of 20 to 59 years may be longer or shorter, the assumed level of pensions may be a higher or lower proportion of the assumed half of net earnings. Pensions may be paid at flat rates or be related to past earnings, they may be financed by taxes on consumption, capital or unearned income and only partially or not at all by levies on earned income and they may be demo grants, state or occupational pensions. However unless the actual, not the nominal, span of working age is extended or the level of pensions is reduced there has to be some redistribution of income from those of working age to those past working age. If the GNP increases in future at the same rate as it has increased in the past the impact of this redistribution will be quite small (see section on Retirement Pensions).

References

Andrews, K. (1993) 'Recovery of patients after four months or more in the persistent vegetative state', *British Medical Journal,* 306(6892), 12 June , pp.1597-1600.

Bissett, B. (ed.) (1993) *House Prices in 1993.* Swindon: Nationwide Building Society, p.3.

Central Policy Review Staff (1977) *Population and the Social Services.* HMSO.

Central Statistical Office (1956) *U.K. Statistical Abstract for 1956.* No.93. HMSO.

Central Statistical Office (1966) *U.K. Statistical Abstract for 1966.* No.103. HMSO.

Eurostat (1991) *Demographic Statistics 1991.* Luxembourg: Office For Official Publications of the European Communities.

Forster, P. (1993) 'The fortysomething barrier: medicine and age discrimination', *British Medical Journal,* 306(6878), 6 March, pp.637-639.

Gillon, R. (1993) 'Patients in the persistent vegetative state: a response to Dr. Andrews', *British Medical Journal,* 306(6892), 12 June, pp.1602-1603.

Kellett, J. (1993) 'Long term care on the NHS: a vanishing prospect', *British Medical Journal,* 306(6881), 27 March.

Office of Population Censuses and Surveys (1991) *Population Trends 66.* HMSO.

The contributors

John Clarke, Emeritus Professor of the University of Durham, is Chairman of the North Durham Health Authority and of the Commission on Population and Environment of the International Union for the Scientific Study of Population. He is Vice-President of the Royal Geographical Society, and was formerly Professor of Geography and Pro-Vice-Chancellor and Sub-Warden in the University of Durham. His research is in the field of population geography.

Brian Holton is currently lecturing in the Department of East Asian Studies at the University of Durham. He has previously taught at the Universities of Edinburgh and Ningbo, China. His research is in the field of Chinese literature, currently focusing on a translation of a major seventeenth century novel. He also takes interest in Buddhist thought.

Robin Humphrey has held research posts in the Rowntree Research Unit at the University of Durham and the Health Care Research Unit at the University of Newcastle upon Tyne, where he is now a lecturer in the Department of Social Policy. His main research interests in the past have been into neighbourhood care and the evaluation of general practice. He is currently researching the social impact of divorce on older people, using Social Network Analysis and the life story approach.

Margot Jefferys, Emeritus Professor of the University of London, is a medical sociologist. She was Director of the Social Research Unit at Bedford College from 1965 to 1982. Her present position is Visiting Professor at the Centre of Medical Law and Ethics, King's College London. She is a Fellow of the Royal College of General Practitioners and a Fellow of the Faculty of Public Health Medicine of the Royal College of Physicians. Her numerous published works include *Growing Old in the Twentieth Century* which she edited for Routledge in 1989 and to which she contributed.

Peter Kaim-Caudle is Emeritus Professor of Social Policy at the University of Durham. He has taught in Universities in Sierra Leone, Ireland, Canada, Fiji, Australia and Taiwan and has written about social policy issues in fourteen countries. He served for many years on the County Durham Social Services Committee, the Durham Executive Council (NHS) and the Central Council for Education and Training in Social Work. He was Chair of the 1988 Local Government Enquiry into National Health Service Provision in the Northern Region, and British Co-Chair of four Sino-British conferences on social policy.

The contributors

Jane Keithley is Director of the Institute of Health Studies at the University of Durham. She is a Registered General Nurse and has for many years been a lecturer in Social Policy. She is a member of Durham Family Health Services Authority. Her teaching and research interests and areas in which she has recently published, include health and health policy, community care, pensions, and the social policy of the European Community.

Yvette Marin is Professor of British Civilisation at the University of Franche-Comté in Besançon, France. She established and is Director of the *Centre de Recherches sur l'Espace Humain et Urbain*). Her main areas of interest are in urban and social studies. She has published *The Gentrification of London* (Didier-Erudition, 1985), a major report on the history of social housing in Britain from its origins to the second World War for the Ministry of Housing in France (July 1992), and numerous articles on British life focusing on housing and social policies. She is a regular contributor to journals and newspapers in France.

Audrey Mullender is Director of the Centre for Applied Social Studies at the University of Durham. She is a qualified social worker with experience as a fieldworker in an area with a high elderly population. Her fifteen-year teaching career has spanned many interests including research on community support for carers of older people and on groupwork initiatives in elderly persons' homes. She has published widely in social work books and journals, here and overseas, and co-authored with David Ward *Self-Directed Groupwork* (Whiting & Birch, 1991).

Ilona Ostner is Professor of Sociology and Gender Studies at the University of Bremen, Germany. She is also the Chairperson of the Centre for Social Policy Research and Head of the Department of Gender and Welfare Studies. She has written and edited eight books, published numerous articles on gender, health and social security, and contributed to several books published in the USA and the UK.

Chris Phillipson is Professor of Applied Social Studies and Social Gerontology at the University of Keele. His publications include *Capitalism and the Construction of Old Age* (1982), *Ageing and Social Policy* (co-editor, 1986), *The Sociology of Old Age* (co-author, 1988), *Changing Work and Retirement* (co-author, 1991) and *Age Barriers at Work* (co-author, 1993).

Barry Thomas is a Senior Lecturer in Economics at the University of Durham. He has taught in several UK universities and has lectured overseas. His publications include books and numerous articles on Economics. His research has included work on economic and social policy for the European Court of Auditors and for the European Commission. He has also acted as a consultant to government agencies and to private sector organisations.

Roger Till is a former Senior Staff Tutor in Extra-Mural Studies at the University of Durham. He has contributed humorous verse to a number of anthologies. On four occasions he was Director of Studies at British Council summer schools in Durham. In earlier years, he was a journalist on newspapers and at the BBC.

Alan Walker is Professor of Social Policy and Chairperson of the Department of Sociological Studies, University of Sheffield. He has been researching and writing on social gerontology for more than 20 years. He is Co-ordinator of the European Community's Observatory on Ageing and Older People and Consultant to the Eurobarometer Study of Attitudes to Ageing.

Lorna Warren is a lecturer in the Institute of Health Studies at the University of Durham. She has been working on studies of the care of older people since 1983. Her particular area of concern is community care, with a focus on domiciliary services and the notion of user/carer involvement. Recent publications cover the experiences of home helps, and neighbourhood support units as a new approach to the social care of older people.

Bill Williamson is Director of the Department of Adult and Continuing Education, University of Durham. He is a sociologist currently undertaking research in adult education. His work centres on the educational needs of people in mining communities and is an extension of previously published work in contemporary British social history. His work in education builds on many years of research on educational opportunity in Britain. His book, *The Temper of the Times: Britain Since World War II* was published by Blackwell in 1990.